## More Praise for *Humble Inquiry*

"An invaluable guide for a consultant trying to understand and untangle system and interpersonal knots. Written with a beguiling simplicity and clarity, it is laden with wisdom and practicality."

**—Irvin Yalom, MD, Professor Emeritus of Psychiatry, Stanford University**

"The lessons contained in this deceptively simple book reach beyond the author's experience gained from a lifetime of consultation to organizations of all sizes and shapes. It provides life lessons for us all. If, as a result of reading this book, you begin to practice the art of humble asking, you will have taken an important step toward living wisely."

**—Samuel Jay Keyser, Peter de Florez Professor Emeritus, MIT**

"This book seriously challenges leaders to re-examine the emphasis on task orientation and 'telling' subordinates how best to do their jobs. Humble Inquiry increases organizational capacity to learn more from cross-cultural teamwork, reduces stress, and increases organizational engagement and productivity."

**—Jyotsna Sanzgiri, MBA, PhD, Professor, California School of Professional Psychology, Alliant International University**

"This book is particularly important for leaders who in these complex times need advice and tools for building trust in their relationships with subordinates individually or in teams."

**—Danica Purg, President, IEDC-Bled School of Management, Bled, Slovenia**

"This book is an exercise in inquiry by a recognized master of humble insight."

**—Art Kleiner, Editor-in-Chief, Booz & Company/*strategy+business***

"Ed Schein has provided a new and thoughtful reframing of interpersonal dynamics through the notion of Humble Inquiry. This short book is packed with insights as Schein rigorously explores the impact of his ideas in his usually clear and readable style."

**—Michael Brimm, Professor of Organizational Behavior, INSEAD Europe**

"*Humble Inquiry* is an elegant treatment of how to go about building and sustaining solid, trusting relationships in or out of the workplace. A masterful take on a critical human skill too infrequently practiced."
    —**John Van Maanen, Erwin Schell Professor of Management and Professor of Organization Studies, MIT**

"A fast read and full of insight! Considering the cultural, occupational, generational, and gender communication barriers we face every day, *Humble Inquiry* proposes a very practical, nonthreatening approach to bridging those gaps and increasing the mutual understanding that leads to operational excellence."
    —**Rosa Antonia Carrillo, MSOD, safety leadership consultant**

"A remarkably valuable guide for anyone interested in leading more effectively and building strong relationships. Ed Schein presents vivid examples grounded in a lifetime of experience as husband, father, teacher, administrator, and consultant."
    —**Robert B. McKersie, Professor Emeritus, Sloan School of Management, MIT**

"Ed Schein has an eye for bold yet subtle insights into the big picture and a knack for writing about them clearly. *Humble Inquiry*—like his previous book *Helping*—shows that he is equally talented at bringing fresh thinking to well-trodden ground."
    —**Grady McGonagill, EdD, Principal, McGonagill Consulting**

"What did I gain from reading *Humble Inquiry*? I became more aware of the subtle but powerful ways we affect each other as we talk and how the right kind of questions can dramatically improve the quality and efficiency of communication, with benefits that range from increased patient safety and satisfaction to employee motivation and morale to organizational performance. You can't afford to not know about this."
    —**Anthony Suchman, MD, MA, University of Rochester School of Medicine and Dentistry**

"With the world as his classroom, Ed Schein continues to guide us through modern day chaos with the powerful behaviors of *Helping* and *Humble Inquiry*. This is a must-read for anyone who truly wishes to achieve important goals!"
    —**Marjorie M. Godfrey, Codirector, The Dartmouth Institute for Health Policy & Clinical Practice Microsystem Academy**

# Humble Inquiry

## Other Books by Edgar Schein

*Organizational Culture and Leadership*

*Helping*

*The Corporate Culture Survival Guide*

*Organizational Psychology*

*Career Anchors*

*Process Consultation*

*DEC Is Dead, Long Live DEC*

# Humble Inquiry

## The Gentle Art of Asking Instead of Telling

**EDGAR H. SCHEIN**

Berrett–Koehler Publishers, Inc.
San Francisco
*a BK Business book*

Berrett-Koehler Publishers, Inc.
1333 Broadway, Suite 1000
Oakland, CA 94612-1921
Tel: (510) 817-2277   Fax: (510) 817-2278   www.bkconnection.com

**Ordering Information**

**Quantity sales.** Special discounts are available on quantity purchases by corporations, associations, and others. For details, contact the "Special Sales Department" at the Berrett-Koehler address above.

**Individual sales.** Berrett-Koehler publications are available through most bookstores. They can also be ordered directly from Berrett-Koehler: Tel: (800) 929-2929; Fax: (802) 864-7626; www.bkconnection.com

**Orders for college textbook/course adoption use.** Please contact Berrett-Koehler. Tel: (800) 929-2929; Fax: (802) 864-7626.

**Orders by U.S. trade bookstores and wholesalers.** Please contact Ingram Publisher Services, Tel: (800) 509-4887; Fax: (800) 838-1149; E-mail: customer .service@ingrampublishingservices.com; or visit www.ingrampublisherservices .com/Ordering for details about electronic ordering.

Berrett-Koehler and the BK logo are registered trademarks of Berrett-Koehler Publishers, Inc.

Printed in the United States of America

Berrett-Koehler books are printed on long-lasting acid-free paper. When it is available, we choose paper that has been manufactured by environmentally responsible processes. These may include using trees grown in sustainable forests, incorporating recycled paper, minimizing chlorine in bleaching, or recycling the energy produced at the paper mill.

**Library of Congress Cataloging-in-Publication Data**

Schein, Edgar H.
Humble inquiry : the gentle art of asking instead of telling / Edgar H. Schein.
 pages  cm
Summary: "From one of the true giants in organizational development, career development and organizational psychology comes a simple and effective technique for building more positive relationships—particularly between people of different status—that will lead to more honest and open interactions and stronger organizations"—Provided by publisher.
 ISBN 978-1-60994-981-5 (pbk.)
 1. Interpersonal communication. 2. Interpersonal relations. 3. Organizational behavior. 4. Humility. I. Title.
 BF637.C45S352   2013
 302.—dc23                                          2013016855

First edition

22  21  20  19  18  17  16            14

cover designed by Susan Malikowski, Designleaf Studio

Produced by BookMatters, copyedited by Tanya Grove, proofed by Anne Smith, indexed by Leonard Rosenbaum.

This book is dedicated to my
main teachers and mentors:
Gordon Allport, Richard Solomon,
David Rioch, Erving Goffman,
Douglas McGregor, and Richard Beckhard.

# Contents

Introduction: Creating Positive Relationships
and Effective Organizations     1

1   Humble Inquiry     7

2   Humble Inquiry in Practice—Case Examples     21

3   Differentiating Humble Inquiry from Other
Kinds of Inquiry     39

4   The Culture of Do and Tell     53

5   Status, Rank, and Role Boundaries as Inhibitors     69

6   Forces Inside Us as Inhibitors     83

7   Developing the Attitude of Humble Inquiry     99

Notes     111

Acknowledgments     113

Index     115

About the Author     119

Author Awards     123

# Introduction: Creating Positive Relationships and Effective Organizations

The motivation to write this book is personal and professional. On the personal level, I have never liked being told things gratuitously, especially things I already know.

The other day I was admiring an unusual bunch of mushrooms that had grown after a heavy rain when a lady walking her dog chose to stop and tell me in a loud voice, "Some of those are poisonous, you know." I replied, "I know," to which she added, "Some of them can kill you, you know."

What struck me was how her need to tell not only made it difficult to respond in a positive manner, but it also offended me. I realized that her tone and her *telling* approach prevented the building of a positive relationship and made further communication awkward. Her motivation might have been to help me, yet I found it unhelpful and wished that she had asked me a question, either at the beginning or after I said "I know," instead of trying to tell me something more.

Why is it so important to learn to ask better questions that help to build positive relationships? Because in an increasingly complex, interdependent, and culturally diverse world, we cannot hope to understand and work with people from different occupational, professional, and national cultures if we do not know how to ask questions and build relationships that are based on mutual respect and the recognition that others know things that we may need to know in order to get a job done.

But not all questions are equivalent. I have come to believe that we need to learn a particular form of questioning that I first called "Humble Inquiry" in my book on *Helping* (2009), and that can be defined as follows:

> **Humble Inquiry** is the fine art of drawing someone out, of asking questions to which you do not already know the answer, of building a relationship based on curiosity and interest in the other person.

The professional motivation to explore Humble Inquiry more extensively comes from the insights I have gained over the past fifty years of consulting with various kinds of organizations. Especially in the high hazard industries in which the problems of safety are paramount, I have learned that good relations and reliable communication across hierarchic boundaries are crucial. In airplane crashes and chemical industry accidents, in the infrequent but serious nuclear plant accidents, in the NASA Challenger and Columbia disasters, and in the British Petroleum gulf spill, a common finding is that lower-ranking employees had information that would have prevented or lessened the consequences of the accident, but either it was not passed up to higher levels, or it was ignored, or it was overridden. When I talk to senior managers, they always assure me that they are open, that they want to hear from their subordinates, and that they take the information seriously. However, when I talk to the subordinates in those same organizations, they tell me either they do not feel safe bringing bad news to their bosses or they've tried but never got any response or even acknowledgment, so they concluded that their input wasn't welcome and gave up. Shockingly often, they settled for risky alternatives rather than upset their bosses with potentially bad news.

When I look at what goes on in hospitals, in operating rooms, and in the health care system generally, I find the same problems of communication exist and that patients frequently pay the price. Nurses and technicians do not feel safe bringing negative information to doctors or correcting a doctor who is about to make a mistake. Doctors will argue that if the others were "professionals" they would speak up, but in many a hospital the nurses will tell you that doctors feel free to yell at nurses in a punishing way, which creates a climate where nurses will certainly not speak up. Doctors engage patients in one-way conversations in which they ask only enough questions to make a diagnosis and sometimes make misdiagnoses because they don't ask enough questions before they begin to tell patients what they should do.

It struck me that what is missing in all of these situations is a climate in which lower-level employees feel safe to bring up issues that need to be addressed, information that would reduce the likelihood of accidents, and, in health care, mistakes that harm patients. How does one produce a climate in which people will speak up, bring up information that is safety related, and even correct superiors or those of higher status when they are about to make a mistake?

The answer runs counter to some important aspects of U.S. culture—*we must become better at asking and do less telling in a culture that overvalues telling.* It has always bothered me how even ordinary conversations tend to be defined by what we *tell* rather than by what we *ask*. Questions are taken for granted rather than given a starring role in the human drama. Yet all my teaching and consulting experience has taught me that what builds a relationship, what solves problems, what moves things forward is *asking the right questions*. In particular, it is the higher-ranking leaders who must learn the art of Humble Inquiry as a first step in creating a climate of openness.

I learned early in my consulting that getting questioning right was more important than giving recommendations or advice and wrote about that in my books on *Process Consultation*.[1] I then realized that giving and receiving help also worked best when the helper asked some questions before giving advice or jumping in with solutions. So I wrote about the importance of asking in my book *Helping*.[2]

I now realize that the issue of asking versus telling is really a fundamental issue in human relations, and that it applies to all of us all the time. What we choose to ask, when we ask, what our underlying attitude is as we ask—all are key to relationship building, to communication, and to task performance.

Building relationships between humans is a complex process. The mistakes we make in conversations and the things we think we should have said after the conversation is over all reflect our own confusion about the balancing of asking and telling, and our automatic bias toward telling. The missing ingredients in most conversations are curiosity and willingness to ask questions to which we do not already know the answer.

It is time to take a look at this form of questioning and examine its role in a wide variety of situations, from ordinary conversations to complex-task performances, such as a surgical team performing an open-heart operation. In a complex and interdependent world, more and more tasks are like a seesaw or a relay race. We tout teamwork and use lots of different athletic analogies, but I chose the seesaw and the relay race to make the point that often it is necessary for *everyone* to do their part. For everyone to do their part appropriately requires good communication; good communication requires building a *trusting relationship;* and building a trusting relationship requires *Humble Inquiry.*

This book is for the general reader, but it has special significance for people in leadership roles because the art of questioning becomes more difficult as status increases. Our culture emphasizes that leaders must be wiser, set direction, and articulate values, all of which predisposes them to tell rather than ask. Yet it is leaders who will need Humble Inquiry most because complex interdependent tasks will require building positive, trusting relationships with subordinates to facilitate good upward communication. And without good upward communication, organizations can be neither effective nor safe.

## About this book

In this book I will first define and explain what I mean by *Humble Inquiry* in Chapter 1. To fully understand *humility*, it is helpful to differentiate three kinds of humility: 1) the humility that we feel around elders and dignitaries; 2) the humility that we feel in the presence of those who awe us with their achievements; and 3) Here-and-now Humility, which results from our being dependent from time to time on someone else in order to accomplish a task that we are committed to. This will strike some readers as academic hairsplitting, but it is the recognition of this third type of humility that is the key to Humble Inquiry and to the building of positive relationships.

To fully explain Humble Inquiry, Chapter 2 will provide a number of short case examples, and Chapter 3 will discuss how this form of questioning is different from other kinds of questions that one may ask.

Chapter 4 will discuss why it is difficult to engage in Humble Inquiry in the kind of task-oriented culture we live in. I label this a "Culture of Do and Tell" and argue that not only do we value *telling* more than *asking*, but we also value *doing* more than *relating* and thereby reduce our capacity and desire to form relationships. Chapter 5 argues that the higher we are in status, the more difficult it becomes to engage in Humble Inquiry while, at the same time, it becomes more important for leaders to learn how to be humble from time to time. Not only do norms and assumptions in our culture make Humble Inquiry difficult, but the complexity of our human brain and the complexity of social relationships also create some constraints and difficulties, which I discuss in Chapter 6.

Finally, in Chapter 7, I provide some suggestions for how we can increase our ability and desire to engage in more Humble Inquiry.

# 1 Humble Inquiry

When conversations go wrong, when our best advice is ignored, when we get upset with the advice that others give us, when our subordinates fail to tell us things that would improve matters or avoid pitfalls, when discussions turn into arguments that end in stalemates and hurt feelings—what went wrong and what could have been done to get better outcomes?

A vivid example came from one of my executive students in the MIT Sloan Program who was studying for his important finance exam in his basement study. He had explicitly instructed his six-year-old daughter not to interrupt him. He was deep into his work when a knock on the door announced the arrival of his daughter. He said sharply, "I thought I told you not to interrupt me." The little girl burst into tears and ran off. The next morning his wife berated him for upsetting the daughter. He defended himself vigorously until his wife interrupted and said, "I sent her down to you to say goodnight and ask you if you wanted a cup of coffee to help with your studying. Why did you yell at her instead of asking her why she was there?"

How can we do better? The answer is simple, but its implementation is not. We would have to do three things: 1) do less telling; 2) learn to do more asking in the particular form of Humble Inquiry; and 3) do a better job of listening and acknowledging. Talking and listening have received enormous attention via hundreds of books on communication. But the social art of asking a question has been strangely neglected.

Yet what we ask and the particular form in which we ask it—what I describe as Humble Inquiry—is ultimately the basis for building trusting relationships, which facilitates better communication and, thereby, ensures collaboration where it is needed to get the job done.

Some tasks can be accomplished by each person doing his or her own thing. If that is the case, building relationships and improving communication may not matter. In the team sports of basketball, soccer, and hockey, teamwork is *desirable* but not essential. But when *all the parties* have to do the right thing—when there is complete, simultaneous interdependence, as in a seesaw or a relay race—then good relationships and open communication become *essential*.

## How Does *Asking* Build Relationships?

We all live in a culture of Tell and find it difficult to ask, especially to ask in a humble way. What is so wrong with telling? The short answer is a sociological one. *Telling* puts the other person down. It implies that the other person does not already know what I am telling and that the other person ought to know it. Often when I am told something that I did not ask about, I find that I already know that and wonder why the person assumes that I don't. When I am told things that I already know or have thought of, at the minimum I get impatient, and at the maximum I get offended. The fact that the other person says, "But I was only trying to help—you might not have thought of it," does not end up being helpful or reassuring.

On the other hand, *asking* temporarily empowers the other person in the conversation and temporarily makes me vulnerable. It implies that the other person knows something that I need to or want to know. It draws the other person into the situation and into the driver's seat; it enables the other person to help or hurt me and, thereby, opens the door to building a relationship. If I don't care about communicating or building a relationship with the other person, then telling is fine. But if part of the goal of the conversation is to *improve* communication and build a relationship, then telling is more risky than asking.

A conversation that leads to a relationship has to be sociologically equitable and balanced. If I want to build a relationship, I have to begin by investing something in it. Humble Inquiry is investing by spending some of my *attention* up front. My question is conveying to the other person, "I am prepared to listen to you and am making myself vulnerable to you." I will get a return on my investment if what the other person tells me is something that I did not know before and needed to know. I will then appreciate being told something new, and a relationship can begin to develop through successive cycles of being told something *in response to asking.*

*Trust* builds on my end because I have made myself vulnerable, and the other person has not taken advantage of me nor ignored me. Trust builds on the other person's end because I have shown an interest in and paid attention to what I have been told. A conversation that builds a trusting relationship is, therefore, an interactive process in which each party invests and gets something of value in return.

All of this occurs within the cultural boundaries of what is considered appropriate good manners and civility. The participants exchange information and attention in successive cycles guided by each of their perceptions of the cultural boundaries of what is appropriate to ask and tell about in the given situation.

Why does this not occur routinely? Don't we all know how to ask questions? Of course we think we know how to ask, but we fail to notice how often even our questions are just another form of telling—rhetorical or just testing whether what we think is right. We are biased toward telling instead of asking because we live in a pragmatic, problem-solving culture in which knowing things and telling others what we know is valued. We also live in a structured society in which building relationships is not as important as task accomplishment, in which it is appropriate and expected that the subordinate does more asking than telling, while the boss does more telling that asking. Having to ask is a sign of weakness or ignorance, so we avoid it as much as possible.

Yet there is growing evidence that many tasks get accomplished better and more safely if team members and especially bosses learn to build relationships through the art of Humble Inquiry. This form of asking shows interest in the other person, signals a willingness to listen, and, thereby, temporarily empowers the other person. It implies a temporary state of dependence on another and, therefore, implies a kind of *Here-and-now Humility*, which must be distinguished from two other forms of humility.

## Three Kinds of Humility

Humility, in the most general sense, refers to granting someone else a higher *status* than one claims for oneself. To be *humiliated* means to be publicly deprived of one's claimed status, to lose face. It is unacceptable in all cultures to humiliate another person, but the rules for what constitutes humiliation vary among cultures due to differences in how status is granted. Therefore, to understand Humble Inquiry, we need to distinguish three kinds of humility based on three kinds of status:

1) *Basic humility*—In traditional societies where status is ascribed by birth or social position, humility is not a choice but a condition. One can accept it or resent it, but one cannot arbitrarily change it. In most cultures the "upper class" is granted an intrinsic respect based on the status one is born into. In Western democracies such as the United States, we are in conflict about how humble to be in front of someone who has been born into it rather than having achieved it. But all cultures dictate the minimum amount of respect required, or the expected politeness and acknowledgment that adults owe each other. We all acknowledge that as human beings we owe each other some basic respect and should act with some measure of civility.

2) *Optional humility*—In societies where status is *achieved* through one's accomplishments, we tend to feel humble in the presence of people who have clearly achieved more than we have, and we either admire or envy them. This is *optional* because we have the choice whether or not to put ourselves in the presence of others who would humble us with their achievements. We can avoid such feelings of humility by the company we choose and who we choose to compare ourselves to, our reference groups. When in the presence of someone whose achievements we respect, we generally know what the expected rules of deference and demeanor are, but these can vary by occupational culture. How to properly show respect for the Nobel Prize–winning physicist or the Olympic Gold Medal–winner may require some coaching by occupational insiders.

3) *Here-and-now Humility*—There is a third kind of

humility that is crucial for the understanding of Humble Inquiry. Here-and-now Humility is how I feel when I am dependent on you. My status is inferior to yours at this moment because you know something or can do something that I need in order to accomplish some task or goal that I have chosen. You have the power to help or hinder me in the achievement of goals that I have chosen and have committed to. I have to be humble because I am temporarily dependent on you. Here I also have a choice. I can either not commit to tasks that make me dependent on others, or I can deny the dependency, avoid feeling humble, fail to get what I need, and, thereby, fail to accomplish the task or unwittingly sabotage it. Unfortunately people often would rather fail than to admit their dependency on someone else.

This kind of humility is easy to see and feel when you are the subordinate, the student, or the patient/client because the situation you are in defines relative status. It is less visible in a team among peers, and it is often totally invisible to the boss who may assume that the formal power granted by the position itself will guarantee the performance of the subordinate. The boss may not perceive his or her dependency on the subordinate, either because of incorrect assumptions about the nature of the task that is being performed or because of incorrect assumptions about a subordinate's level of commitment to the particular job. The boss may assume that if something is in the subordinate's job description, it will be done, and not notice the many ways in which subordinates will withhold information or drift off what they have been trained for. But, if I am a boss on a seesaw or in a relay race in which everyone's performance matters to getting the job done at all, I am de facto dependent on the subordinate whether I recognize it or not. Getting the seesaw to move and passing the baton will work only if all the participants, regardless of formal status, recognize their dependence on each other. It is in that situation where Humble Inquiry by all the parties becomes most relevant, where the humility is not based on a priori status gaps or differences in prior achievement, but on recognized here-and-now interdependence.

When you are dependent on someone to get a task accomplished, it is essential that you build a relationship with that person that will lead to open task-related communication. Consider two possibilities. You are the boss in the relay race. *Telling* the person to put out her or his left hand so that you, who are right-handed, can easily pass the baton, may or may not lead to effective passing. However, if you decide to engage in Humble Inquiry prior to the race, you might ask your teammate's preference for which hand to use. You might then discover that the person has an injured left hand that does not work as well, and it would be better for you to pass with *your* left.

Shouldn't the subordinate have mentioned that before the race anyway? Not if in that culture for one person to speak up directly to a person of higher status is taboo. If the baton pass is an instrument a nurse passes to the surgeon, isn't it enough for the surgeon to *tell* the nurse what she needs and expect a correct response? Ordinarily yes, but what if the nurse is temporarily distracted by a beep from monitoring equipment or confused because of a possible language problem or thinks it is the wrong instrument? Should he not speak up and admit that he does not understand, or are the cultural forces in the situation such that he will guess and maybe make a costly mistake? If, in the culture of that operating room, the doctors are gods and one simply does not question or confront them, that nurse will not speak up, even if there is potential harm to the patient. My point is that in both of those examples, the boss and the doctor are de facto dependent on their subordinates and must, therefore, recognize their Here-and-now Humility. Failure to do so and failure to engage in Humble Inquiry to build a relationship *prior to the race or the operation itself* then leads to poor performance, potential harm, and feelings of frustration all around.

When such situations occur within a given culture where the rules of deference and demeanor are clear, there is a chance that the parties will understand each other. But when the team members in an interdependent task are more multicultural, both the language and the set of behavioral rules about how to deal with authority and trust may vary. To make this clear, let's look at a hypothetical multicultural example from medicine, keeping in mind that the same cultural forces would operate in a comparable example of a task force in a business or in a curriculum committee in a school.

## THREE KINDS OF HUMILITY—
## A SURGICAL TEAM EXAMPLE

Consider these three types of humility in the context of a hypothetical British hospital operating room where a complex operation is being performed. The surgeon is Dr. Roderick Brown, the son of Lord Brown, who is a respected senior surgeon and works with the Royal Family; the anesthesiologist is Dr. Yoshi Tanaka, recently arrived from Japan on a residency fellowship; the surgical nurse is Amy Grant, an American working in the United Kingdom because her husband has a job there; and the surgical tech is Jack Swift, who is from a lower-class section of London and has gone as high as he is likely to go at the hospital.[3]

All the members of the team would feel some *basic humility* with respect to the surgeon, Dr. Brown, except possibly Amy, who does not particularly respect the British class structure. Both Amy and Dr. Tanaka would feel *optional humility* with respect to Dr. Brown because they can see how talented Brown is with surgical tools. Jack is likely to feel such *optional humility* with respect to all the others in the room. What none of them may be sufficiently aware of is that they are *interdependent* and will, therefore, have to experience *Here-and-now Humility* from time to time with respect to each other.

Dr. Brown, the senior surgeon, may know implicitly, but would not necessarily acknowledge openly, that he is also dependent on the other three. A situation might well arise where he needs information or something to be done by the others in the room who have lower status than he. In the context of the task to be done, situations will arise where an occupationally higher-status person temporarily has lower status by virtue of being dependent and, therefore, should display Here-and-now Humility to ensure a better performance and a safer outcome for the patient.

The higher-status person often denies or glosses this kind of dependency by rationalizing that "I am, after all, working with professionals." That implies that they are all competent, are committed to the superordinate goals of healing the patient, and accept their roles and relative status in the room. It implies that they don't feel humiliated by having orders barked at them or having help demanded of them. Their "professionalism" also typically assumes that they will not humiliate the person with higher status by offering criticism or help unless asked. The burden then falls on the higher-status person to ask for help and *to create the climate that gives permission for the help to be given.*

**Situational Trouble or Surprise.** If things work smoothly, there may be no issues around status and open communication. But what if something goes wrong or something unexpected occurs? For example, if Dr. Tanaka is about to make a major mistake on the anesthetics, and the nurse, Amy, notices it, what should she do? Should she speak up? And what are the consequences of her speaking up about it? Being American, she might just blurt it out and risk that Dr. Tanaka would, in fact, be humiliated by being corrected by a lower-status nurse, a woman, and an American.

If the corrective comment was made by Dr. Brown, it might be embarrassing, but would have been accepted because the senior person can legitimately correct the junior person. Dr. Tanaka might actually appreciate it. Jack might have seen the potential error but would not feel licensed to speak up at all. If Amy or the tech made the mistake, they might get yelled at and thrown off the team because from the point of view of the senior doctor, they could easily be replaced by someone more competent.

What if Dr. Brown was about to make a mistake, would anyone tell him? Dr. Tanaka has learned in his culture that one *never* corrects a superior. This might go so far as to cover up for a surgeon's mistake in order to protect the face of the superior and the profession. Amy would experience conflict and might or might not speak up depending on how psychologically safe she felt in the situation. That might be based on what kind of history of communication and relationship she had with Dr. Brown and other male surgeons in her past career. She might not know whether Dr. Brown would be humiliated by having a nurse offer a corrective comment or question. And humiliation must be avoided in most cultures, so it would be difficult for her to speak up unless she and Dr. Brown had built a relationship in which she felt safe to do so.

Jack would certainly not speak up but might later tell terrible stories about Dr. Brown to his tech colleagues if the operation went badly and the patient was harmed or died unnecessarily. If this incident later led to an official inquiry, Jack and Dr. Tanaka might be called as witnesses. They might be asked what they had observed and would either have to lie or, if they admitted that they saw the mistake, might be criticized for not having done anything at the time.

All this would result from Dr. Brown (the leader) being insensitive to the cultural rules around speaking up across status boundaries and not doing anything to change those rules within his surgical team. What is missing in this scenario, and it is often missing in all kinds of complex interdependent tasks, is a social mechanism that overrides the barriers to communication across status lines where humiliation is a cultural possibility. To build this social mechanism—a relationship that facilitates relevant, task-oriented, open communication across status boundaries—requires that leaders learn the art of Humble Inquiry. The most difficult part of this learning is for persons in the higher-status position to become Here-and-now Humble, to realize that in many situations *they are de facto dependent on subordinates and other lower-status team members.*

This kind of humility is difficult to learn because in achievement-oriented cultures where knowledge and the display of it are admired, being Here-and-now Humble implies loss of status. Yet this is precisely the kind of humility that will increasingly be needed by leaders, managers, and professionals of all sorts because they will find themselves more and more in tasks where mutual interdependency is the basic condition. That might at times require leaders to ask their team, "Am I doing this correctly? Tell me if I am doing something wrong." This is even harder to learn when some of the members of the team come from traditional cultures in which arbitrary status lines must not be overridden and where task failure is preferable to humiliation and loss of face.

What would it take to get Dr. Tanaka, Amy, and even Jack to confront Dr. Brown when he is about to make a mistake? Efforts to define common goals, require procedures such as checklists, and standardize training are necessary but not sufficient because, in a new and ambiguous situation, team members will fall back on their own cultural rules and do unpredictable things. A leader of any multicultural team who really wanted to ensure open task-related communication would use Humble Inquiry to first build a relationship with the others that would make them feel psychologically safe and able to overcome the conflict they may experience between their duties and their culturally and professionally defined sense of deference.

## What Is Inquiry?

Having defined what *humility* means in this analysis of Humble Inquiry, we need next to ask what *inquiry* means. Inquiry is also a complex concept. Questioning is both a science and an art. Professional question askers such as pollsters have done decades of research on how to ask a question to get the kind of information they want. Effective therapists, counselors, and consultants have refined the art of questioning to a high degree. But most of us have not considered how questions should be asked in the context of daily life, ordinary conversations, and, most importantly, task performance. When we add the issue of asking questions across cultural and status boundaries, things become very muddy indeed.

What we ask, how we ask it, where we ask it, and when we ask it all matter. But the essence of Humble Inquiry goes beyond just overt questioning. The kind of inquiry I am talking about derives from an *attitude of interest and curiosity*. It implies a desire to build a relationship that will lead to more open communication. It also implies that one makes oneself vulnerable and, thereby, arouses positive helping behavior in the other person. Such an attitude is reflected in a variety of behaviors other than just the specific questions we ask. Sometimes we display through body language and silence a curiosity and level of interest that gets the other person talking even when we have said nothing.

Feelings of Here-and-now Humility are, for the most part, the basis of curiosity and interest. If I feel I have something to learn from you or want to hear from you some of your experiences or feelings because I care for you, or need something from you to accomplish a task, this makes me temporarily dependent and vulnerable. It is precisely my temporary subordination that creates psychological safety for you and, therefore, increases the chances that you will tell me what I need to know and help me get the job done. If you exploit the situation and lie to me or take advantage of me by selling me something I don't need or giving me bad advice, I will learn to avoid you in the future or punish you if I am your boss. If you tell me what I need to know and help me, we have begun to build a positive relationship.

Inquiry, in this context, does imply that you ask questions. But not any old question. The dilemma in U.S. culture is that we don't really distinguish what I am defining as Humble Inquiry carefully enough from *leading* questions, *rhetorical* questions, *embarrassing* questions, or statements in the form of questions—such as journalists seem to love— which are deliberately provocative and intended to put you down. If leaders, managers, and all kinds of professionals are to learn Humble Inquiry, they will have to learn to differentiate carefully among the possible questions to ask and make choices that build the relationship. How this is done will vary with the setting, the task, and the local circumstances, as we will see in later chapters.

In the next chapter, I want first to provide a wide range of examples of Humble Inquiry to make clear what I mean by it and to illustrate how varied the behavior can be depending on the situation and the context.

## QUESTIONS FOR THE READER

- Think about various people whom you admire and respect. What is the type of humility that you feel in each case?

- Think about tasks that require collaboration. In what way are you dependent on another person? Try to reflect on and recognize the temporary Here-and-now Humility that is required of each of you as you help each other. Do you think you can talk about this kind of humility with each other when you next discuss your joint task? If not, why not?

- Now think about yourself in your daily life with friends and family. Reflect on the kinds of questions you tend to ask in ordinary conversation and in task situations. Are they different? Why?

- What is the one most important thing you have learned about how to ask questions?

- Now take a few minutes just to reflect quietly on what you have learned in general so far.

# 2

## Humble Inquiry in Practice— Case Examples

In this chapter I present a wide range of examples from the mundane to the profound to illustrate that there is no absolute formula for Humble Inquiry. Remember: *Humble Inquiry is the skill and the art of drawing someone out, of asking questions to which you do not already know the answer, of building a relationship based on curiosity and interest in the other person.*

It is an attitude reflected in a variety of behaviors that are appropriate to the given situation. Many of the examples do not involve actual interdependence but illustrate the importance of building relationships such that when you are suddenly interdependent, the other party will trust you enough to be open and helpful. Ultimately the purpose of Humble Inquiry is to build relationships that lead to trust which, in turn, leads to better communication and collaboration.

### 1. Taking Mary to tea

(A missed opportunity to Humbly Inquire)

I had arrived in Cambridge with my new bride and was getting ready to teach my first class ever, a lecture course on social psychology for first-year MBA students. Most evenings I was deep at work on my lectures because I was so anxious about my first teaching performance.

Mary asked me several times if I'd take a break and maybe take her out for a cup of tea, to which I replied that I was sorry, but I had to finish the lecture.

Looking back on this scene I feel sad, regretful, and somewhat ashamed. What should I have done? I have a caring attitude and I wanted to be helpful, but I wanted to finish the lectures. Going out to tea would have been a total disruption. In reflecting back on this event I realize that I had three options.

**Option 1**  Stick to my guns, politely and firmly say, "Sorry, can't right now," and continue to work on the lecture. This is what I did and now regret.

Problems with this option:

- It put Mary down, telling her that my work was more important than she was.
- Mary might have needed to discuss a problem and wanted my input; if so, I would not have learned about it and, therefore, would not have helped.
- I felt guilty and ashamed.
- I built up some resentment because I felt guilty or ashamed.

**Option 2**  Give in and take Mary out to tea.

Problems with this option:

- I might go out for tea physically but not psychologically, so it would be tense, awkward, and unsatisfying to both of us.
- I might enjoy it but then have to work later and, thereby, create new problems.

- I might resent it and unconsciously punish Mary in some way.
- I might develop an image of Mary as "always asking."
- Mary might not have wanted a tea break but needed to talk to me about something and used tea as a vehicle.
- Mary might have felt guilty for interrupting me.

**Option 3** Humble Inquiry—Be empathic, sit down with Mary for a moment and give her my full attention. Ask her in a kind and attentive way what's on her mind and suggest that we talk for a minute. In retrospect, this is what I should I have done.

Why this option?

- By seriously asking, I would have been honoring the relationship, honoring her request for attention, and avoiding the put-down.
- I would have had a chance of finding out whether she just needed a break, needed to get out of the house, or needed to talk over some important issue with me.
- I then would have had the information to decide whether my lecture or Mary's need was more important at that moment and could have made the appropriate decision.
- We could then decide *together* whether to have tea then, to talk then, to have tea later, to talk later, etc. It would have been the appropriate next step, and that would have contributed to building the relationship.
- I would have had a chance to share my anxiety about the forthcoming lectures and enabled Mary to gain some empathy for my situation and offer help.
- I would then feel that the break was worth taking even if it cost me some work time.

**WHAT I LEARNED**

- When the choice is between *you* or *me*, look for a way to explore *us*, the relationship itself.
- Ask an open question to get information that you need (a question that is not answerable with just a yes or no).
- When one is too busy with one's own agenda but wants to display a caring attitude, what often works best is a *small change* in behavior, not a total revision of the relationship.
- A small change allows a *brief* interruption to get more information before making a big decision.
- The small change should invite *joint* problem solving.
- Small changes *now* avoid the need for big changes *later*.
- Humble Inquiry would have enabled a small change.

## 2. Getting departmental telephone costs down
(Using Humble Inquiry to get help from subordinates)

When I was the chair of my department of fifteen professors, I got a note from my dean that our phone costs were way out of line. I was *told* that I should find out what the problem was and get the costs down. I received a packet of information which provided a list of all the calls made by each faculty member, presumably to help me locate the problem persons and get them into line. So my job was to figure out what form of inquiry would yield the best result in terms of solving the problem.

**Option 1** Go over with each professor her or his list of calls and find out which ones were legitimate and which were not.

Problems with this option:

- This would involve *telling* people they had a cost overrun problem and requiring a detailed explanation.

▪ This option would offend people, make them defensive, and actually reduce the chances of finding out what was really going on.

**Option 2** Go over the list myself, locate cases that looked out of line to me, and selectively call faculty members for explanations.

　　Problems with this option:

▪ This option would be very time consuming.

▪ I would still run the risk of creating defensiveness.

▪ My relationship with the faculty members would be undermined.

**Option 3—(Humble Inquiry)** Focus on the goal of reducing the telephone bill without destroying my relationships with my faculty. For *me* to know who had gone out of line and why was not really important. To implement this option I asked my secretary to send each faculty member his or her list of calls accompanied by my memo saying that the Dean had told me that our costs were out of line. The memo then *asked* each faculty member to 1) look at her or his own list of calls to 2) determine whether he or she had calls that should have been on other accounts and 3) to monitor this in the future. I made it clear that I was not interested in looking at each list and that I trusted each faculty member to examine and correct telephone usage in his or her own office. Though it was quite prescriptive, it was, in effect, asking them to help me in solving the dean's problem of cost overruns.

　　The important issue was for me to realize that I was dependent on them for the relevant information and to figure out what form of questioning would yield the best result in terms of solving the problem and, at the same time, enhancing the trust level between me and the faculty rather than risking offense and, thereby, reducing the trust level. Such offense could easily have resulted if every faculty member thought I was going over all his calls individually.

Why this option?

- It demonstrates my trust in faculty members to examine and correct telephone usage on their own, rather than risking offense and, thereby, reducing the trust level.
- It is, in effect, *asking* them to help me in solving the dean's problem of cost overruns.

## WHAT I LEARNED

- I had to reflect carefully on what I was really trying to do in a supervisory role before leaping into action.
- I had to accept my dependency on others for the relevant information and be Here-and-now Humble, i.e., ask the faculty for help instead of telling them what to do.
- I had to figure out what kind of question would really provide the answer, and, more importantly, how to ask that question—in this case through a memo that also let people know that I was not interested in individual information.

The method I ended up with did lead to several faculty letting me know that they had found out that some graduate students had made all kinds of long distance calls that should not have been on the department account. I felt good that they could come to me to tell me what they were doing rather than my having to ask them to tell me what they were doing.

## 3. A CEO asks a tough question

At a top management meeting to discuss succession plans for several senior positions, the following conversation took place:

> **Head of HR:** "I think one of our best candidates to be put into the pipeline for the CEO position after you (the present CEO) retire is Joe. He has had good international experience and only needs a few more years in the New York headquarters to see how the whole system works.
>
> **A member of the management development staff:** "I recently talked to Joe and learned that he has young children he wants to educate in Germany, so he has been lobbying to be transferred to the German subsidiary where he would like to spend the next five years. He is quite adamant about getting back to Germany. I know he does not want to stay here."
>
> **CEO:** "That really poses a problem because he really needs the experience here in New York if he is to develop into CEO potential."
>
> **HR:** "I guess we should then take him off the succession ladder."
>
> **CEO:** "Let me talk to him before we do that."
>
> **This triggered my concerns that the CEO would bully him into staying and would risk having a very unhappy subordinate. So I spoke up.**
>
> **Ed:** "If he has made it clear that he wants to go to Germany for his next assignment, shouldn't we honor that wish?" (Humble Inquiry)
>
> **CEO:** "Ed, I have to talk to him because we owe him a full disclosure of his situation. I will not try to

convince him or use power tactics, but I feel I need to tell him that if he does not stay on in New York, we will have to take him off the succession track. That is a piece of information we owe him. It would not be fair to take him off the track without telling him. He can then decide how to balance his work and family priorities. For example, he might want to move the family back and commute or find some other adaptation. But he needs to know the reality which is what I have to convey to him and then ask him what he wants to do." (Humble Inquiry)

**Option 1**  Take Joe off the succession ladder.

Problems with this option:

- They would have to find another viable candidate for the position.
- Joe may be the best person for the job but wouldn't be given that chance.

**Option 2**  Give Joe the full information and ask him (Humble Inquiry) what he wants to do. Allow Joe to decide how to balance his work and family priorities.

Why this option:

- Although it's possible that the CEO might bully Joe into staying and risk having an unhappy subordinate, Joe deserves to know the truth: that if he does not stay in New York, he will be taken off the succession track.
- Joe might find a workable solution, such as moving his family to Germany and commuting to New York.
- It asks Joe for a decision (Humble Inquiry) rather than making the decision for him.

**WHAT I LEARNED**

- Taking people off the promotion ladder without telling them is showing less respect and being more authoritarian than making oneself vulnerable by engaging in conversation.

- That I could easily fall into the trap of telling, i.e., making the decision for Joe, and fail to ask where asking was appropriate.

## 4. I launch a new task force
and use Humble Inquiry to get commitment

I was on the board of a local environmental organization that wanted to launch a capital fundraising campaign. the executive director, Joan, and her Executive Committee of the Board, asked me to chair a task force whose job would be to determine if the board was emotionally ready to launch a Capital Campaign. We asked eight of the more active board members to join the task force. The next step was to have our first meeting to decide what to do. Joan had been through a previous Capital Campaign ten years earlier and felt that many mistakes had been made. She proposed that at the beginning of the meeting she brief the group on the previous campaign's mistakes.

**Option 1** Start out by *telling* the group about previous mistakes to help them avoid going in wrong directions.

Problems with this option:

- *Telling* the group anything would focus attention on Joan and me, rather than on us as a group.

- By starting with potential problems, it would put a negative slant on the Capital Campaign from the beginning.

- Some members had been involved in the previous campaign and might get defensive.

**Option 2** Start with an informal dinner meeting and begin to build a relationship with the group members by *asking* each person the question: "Why does each of you belong to this organization in the first place?" (Humble Inquiry). Have each member around the table answer the question with no interruptions, questions, or comments until all ten have spoken. This is what we did with great success in that most members were very positive and enthusiastic about the organization and its future.

Why this option?

- The rules and the nature of the question introduce an atmosphere of inquiry and put emphasis on positive feelings about the organization.
- This allows each person to speak openly about the organization, making it clear at the outset whether there would be enough enthusiasm and energy to launch the Capital Campaign.
- Having each member answer the questions builds a sense of shared responsibility and unifies the group.

**WHAT I LEARNED**

- When a question is asked in a *group* setting, it is important to impose a rule that everyone gets to answer the question before back-and-forth discussion is allowed.
- A question should elicit information and feelings important to the group's mission.
- It is indeed crucial to start the meeting with everyone speaking from the heart before any interaction is allowed.
- The chair should control the process, not the content.

The next four examples illustrate a more spontaneous use of Humble Inquiry and show how that can have powerful and often unanticipated effects.

## 5. Giving directions

My house was on a street that feeds directly onto the main highway into Boston. I was in my front garden when a woman drove up and asked me whether I could direct her to Massachusetts Avenue. This would have meant turning around and going back across several streets. I asked her, "Where are you trying to get?" (Humble Inquiry). She replied that she was trying to get to downtown Boston. She was already on the direct road to Boston, so I told her to just keep going on the road she was on. To this day I wonder what would have happened to her if I had told her how to get to Massachusetts Ave.

### WHAT I LEARNED

- Don't jump in telling answers until you know what the other person really needs to know.
- Don't assume that the person with the question has asked the right question.

## 6. Initiating culture change
(an unexpected consulting success)

This case study is an example of how an innocent Humble Inquiry can initiate a change process.

The CEO of a power company wanted me to help launch a culture change project because he felt that the organization was stuck in an old and obsolete set of practices and norms. Would I come to diagnose and then propose change steps? I did not know much about this organization or the CEO's perceptions or motivations, so I inquired whether he would be willing to come visit me first to define the problem (Humble Inquiry). I was very curious about his motivations and did not want to get involved in a visit before I knew what he wanted.

He and his COO and head of organization development decided that this was a good idea and agreed to spend a half-day with me at my house. When we sat ourselves down in my garden I took an inquiring attitude (Humble Inquiry) and waited for them to tell me what was on their mind. They launched into a series of general statements about how this old company had a culture that was immovable and frustrating. My interest and curiosity grew, but I could not get a sense of what they were talking about because it was too general. I was feeling *ignorant* of what they meant by *stuck* and *immovable*. When feeling this way, I have found that one of the best kinds of Humble Inquiry is just to *ask for an example*, which is what I did.

The COO jumped in with the following: "Just yesterday I had one of my regular staff meetings of my group of 15 members of the leadership team. They *always sit in the same seats* around this huge table. Yesterday, there were only five people at the meeting and *they again sat in their same seats* even though that scattered them all around the room. It was really crazy . . . you see what we are up against?"

He then looked at me expectantly, presumably hoping for affirmation and support. I had many choices of how to respond. (You should ask yourself what you might have said at this moment.) Spontaneously—because I was genuinely curious—I asked, "What did you do?" (Humble Inquiry)

He said, "I did not do anything." (Missed opportunity)

And in that moment a huge light bulb went off in his

head and in the heads of the CEO and the VP of organization development. My innocent question revealed that whatever problems they were having with stodginess in their own culture, it was supported and reinforced by their own inaction. For the next two hours, the four of us explored all the ways in which they were colluding in maintaining what they were complaining about and how they could change their own behavior. Over the next year they were able to make most of the culture changes that they desired, all triggered by the reframing of their own role through my humble question.

What could the COO have done at the moment? Humble Inquiry on his part would have been to say to the group in a curious and nonpunitive way, "Why are you sitting so far away?"

### WHAT I LEARNED

- Asking for examples is not only one of the most powerful ways of showing curiosity, interest, and concern, but also—and even more important—it clarifies general statements.
- A timely open question is sometimes all that is needed to start effective problem solving.

## 7. A job definition problem

(the power of ignorance)

I was working with Shell Australia and was invited to join the senior management for lunch. In the middle of the lunch, the CEO brought up the news that they were losing their VP of administration. The CEO said he hoped that I would not mind if they did a little company business during lunch and launched into the issue by announcing that Peter, the primary candidate, seemed like a perfectly OK candidate to promote into that job, what did the others think? Several of the VPs were clearly nervous about Peter. They discussed his strengths but somehow continued to feel uncomfortable about him. They were all *telling* why Peter was not right for the job.

I watched this for a while and became puzzled why they seemed to like Peter but could not resolve giving him the job. I also got curious about what a VP of admin did in this organization, so I asked: "What does the VP of administration do?" (Humble Inquiry)

I got a few patronizing smiles but then they decided to take the time to answer the question. "He has finance, accounting, personnel, long-range planning, public relations—"

At this moment one of VPs said that it was in public Relations that Peter had problems—he was a good inside guy but not effective externally. They immediately agreed on this as the reason they were nervous about giving Peter the job.

And then one of them asked, "Does PR have to be part of this job? In fact, isn't it getting to be such a big issue in Australia with all the new environmental issues that we should have a VP of just PR?" (Humble Inquiry plus suggestion). The group agreed immediately to separate out PR and then agreed further that Peter was perfect for the other functions. Problem solved.

### WHAT I LEARNED

- Accessing your ignorance, or allowing curiosity to lead you, is often the best guide to what to ask about.
- Once again, asking for an example (what does the VP of admin do?) proved to be crucial to problem solving.

## 8. The sympathetic oncologist

(providing choices)

When my wife Mary had her first bout of breast cancer in her 50s, we were sent to an oncologist who immediately conveyed to her an interest in her total personality and life situation through body language (intense attention and eye contact), through taking lots of time with questions, and always responding sympathetically (Humble Inquiry attitude). He asked her several general and personal questions before zeroing in on the medically related issues. My wife felt respected as a total human being and, therefore, felt more open in voicing her concerns about treatment.

When it came time to planning treatment, he told us that there were several combinations of chemo and radiation that were possible and were equally likely to be beneficial and left the door wide open as to what might work best for us (Humble Inquiry). He asked what our travel plans were for the following year. We mentioned several long trips that were on the books and the fact that we spend the winter months in California. He immediately told us that we should not change any of our plans and that whatever treatment was needed could be scheduled around our trips and could be delivered as well in California.

What was striking was his questioning us about our other life priorities, which made Mary feel she could trust him totally. This increased her motivation to accept his prescription and work hard on her treatment. She went into remission for ten years, but another cancer grew and it was very important to her to have the same oncologist. He was available, so all went well on that round. After another 15 years of remission, the cancer surfaced once again. This time the same oncologist was not available, and it was immediately evident that the new doctor was more technical in orientation and much less interested in how treatment would fit into our total life situation. The result was much more anxiety and worry on Mary's part, which led to searching out a second opinion and shifting to another doctor, who was again more personal and was able to make Mary more comfortable even though the prognosis was worse.

**WHAT I LEARNED**

- In contrasting the doctors, it was striking to me how quickly Humble Inquiry created a comfortable relationship and how quickly the absence of it created anxiety and worry.
- Humble Inquiry was conveyed by the whole attitude, not just the specific questions that the doctor asked.
- The questions that were most important in establishing the relationship were personal ones, not technical/medical ones.

## In Summary

All of the examples above are intended to either illustrate an attitude or provide specific questions that show interest and respect, which will stimulate more truth telling and collaboration. As the quality of communication increases, the task is accomplished better. These cases also illustrate that Humble Inquiry is not a checklist to follow or a set of prewritten questions—it is behavior that comes out of respect, genuine curiosity, and the desire to improve the quality of the conversation by stimulating greater openness and the sharing of task-relevant information.

## QUESTIONS FOR THE READER

- Think about a conversation in which you were the subordinate or had a lower status than the other person and felt respected and acknowledged. Can you identify what the other person did to make you feel that way?

- Think about a situation in which you were the boss or the person with higher status and a conversation with a subordinate went very well. Think about another situation that went badly. Compare your behavior in both cases. What might account for the difference?

- Now take a few minutes just to reflect quietly on what you have learned in general so far.

# 3

## Differentiating Humble Inquiry from Other Forms of Inquiry

One of the best ways to understand Humble Inquiry is to position it relative to some other forms of inquiry. We have a tendency to think of asking or telling as just simple alternatives when, in fact, there are many forms of each with different consequences. In this chapter I want to make clear how Humble Inquiry differs from several other kinds of inquiry that appear to be very similar but actually control the flow of the conversation more than one might want to do in a given situation.

### Four Forms of Inquiry

It is not enough to decide, "OK, instead of always *telling,* I am going to be more *inquiring,*" because there are so many ways of inquiring. As I enter a conversation and attempt to build a relationship, I should be aware of the choices I have in *how* I inquire and to understand that some seemingly very open ways of inquiring are actually quite controlling of the other person. If we really want to get the other person's full story, we have to avoid steering the conversation inadvertently.

In the analysis of how to be helpful to another person, I distinguish four fundamentally different forms of inquiry which will be useful in this analysis:[4]

1) Humble Inquiry

2) Diagnostic inquiry

3) Confrontational inquiry

4) Process-oriented inquiry

## HUMBLE INQUIRY

Humble Inquiry maximizes my curiosity and interest in the other person and minimizes bias and preconceptions about the other person. I want to *access my ignorance* and ask for information in the least biased and threatening way. I do not want to lead the other person or put him or her into a position of having to give a socially acceptable response. I want to inquire in the way that will best discover what is really on the other person's mind. I want others to feel that I accept them, am interested in them, and am genuinely curious about what is on their minds regarding the particular situation we find ourselves in.

A dramatic example of this is how Ken Olsen, the founder of Digital Equipment Corporation, used to wander around the company, stop at an engineer's desk, and ask: "What are you working on?" Because Ken was genuinely interested, the pair would end up in a long conversation that would be satisfying both technically and personally. Even when the company had over 100,000 people worldwide, Ken was well known and loved because so many people had experienced him as a humble inquirer. This love was especially surprising because Ken could also frequently fall into the telling mode and be brutal and tyrannical. We take it for granted that the boss is always telling us things, we expect that; genuine interest from the boss is much rarer and much more appreciated.

Does such inquiry have to be sincere? Can we simulate interest and get credit for being caring if we don't have the feeling or attitude that Humble Inquiry demands? Humans are very sensitive creatures and we send many signals of which we are not aware (as I discuss further in Chapter 6). In talking to many subordinates in organizations, I find that the insincere boss is spotted very quickly and often resented. I suspect, therefore, that if I am not really interested, the other person will sense it, no matter how I phrase my questions. This means that all kinds of questions, even some kinds of *telling* can be Humble Inquiry if the motive behind the behavior is sincere interest. That interest will be conveyed in body language, tone of voice, timing, and other cues.

As the examples in Chapter 2 show, Humble Inquiry comes across differently depending on the situation. Conversations always occur within a set of cultural rules, and it is, therefore, not desirable to try to develop standard categories of questions that do or do not qualify as Humble Inquiry. What can be said is that whatever you do when you try to humbly inquire, try to minimize your own preconceptions, clear your mind at the beginning of the conversation, and maximize your listening as the conversation proceeds. In fact, the most important diagnostic that the other person will use to decide whether or not you are interested is not only what you ask but also how well you hear the response. Your attitude and motive will then reveal themselves in your further questions and responses as the conversation proceeds.

How Humble Inquiry plays out also depends on the assumptions the two parties make about the purpose of the conversation, their relative status, and the degree to which they already have a relationship. If they encounter each other as strangers in a neutral situation, such as at a cocktail party, the conversation itself becomes an exploration of how much each person can claim that the other will acknowledge and accept. If I choose not to tell but to approach the other in a Humble Inquiry manner, I will either stay silent or begin with something neutral like, "Hello, my name is Ed Schein. What is your name?" The ritual dance then begins with alternate telling and acknowledging. If I become interested and choose to remain in the Humble Inquiry mode I will emphasize exploratory questions that minimize my telling and maximize letting the other person tell his or her story in as unbiased a way as possible.

Examples of how to get the conversation started and keep it going:

"So . . ." (with an expectant look)

"What's happening?"

"What's going on?"

"What brings you here?

"Go on . . ."

"Can you give me an example?"

Paradoxically, "Hi, how are you?" does not qualify as Humble Inquiry because it is culturally scripted to elicit "Fine, how are you?" I have observed that the only time I tell others how I *really* am is when they say something less scripted, such as "How are things going?" and add an expectant look. Within a given culture, participants know when they are asked a scripted question and know to give a scripted answer. We all learn many kinds of scripted inquiries that are not really meant to elicit a sincere response. This can become problematic when the cultures involved have different rules. In my executive classes at MIT, the U.S. students sometimes sincerely asked Japanese colleagues to dinner with "Can you come to dinner next Saturday?" and received a yes answer only to find that no one showed up. We learned that the Japanese were scripted to answer yes, which meant "I have understood your invitation" but did not mean "Yes, I will come." We further learned that it was necessary and OK to follow up with "Please come to our house. Will you be able to come at 6:30?"

To summarize these points and to sharpen the distinction between Humble Inquiry and the forms of inquiry which I discuss next: Humble Inquiry does not influence either the content of what the other person has to say, nor the form in which it is said.

## DIAGNOSTIC INQUIRY

One of the most common deviations from Humble Inquiry occurs when I get curious about a particular thing the other person is telling me and choose to focus on it. I am not *telling* with this kind of question, but I am steering the conversation and influencing the other person's mental process in unknown ways. This was illustrated in my earlier example of giving directions when someone asked me how to get to Massachusetts Avenue and I responded with "Where are you trying to get?" I was steering the conversation, but because I had been asked for help, I thought of this as still Humble Inquiry, though I was running the risk that the other person might say, "none of your business."

What differentiates this form of inquiry is that it influences the other's *mental process*. By asking a further question instead of answering the original question, I am taking charge of the direction of the conversation and must, therefore, consider whether or not this is desirable. The main issue is whether this steering is in the interest of getting the job done, as was my question, or is it indulging my curiosity in an inappropriate way? An example of such indulgence would be if I asked, "*Why* are you trying to get to Massachusetts Aveue?"

This form of inquiry which influences the client's mental *process* can be further classified by what the questioner's diagnostic focus is.

**1) Feelings and Reactions**—questions which focus others on their feelings and reactions in response to the events they have described or the problems that have been identified

Examples:

"How did (do) you *feel* about that?"

"Did (does) that arouse any *reactions* in you?"

"What was (is) your emotional *reaction* to that?"

As innocent and supportive as these questions might seem, they take control of the situation and force others to think about something that they may not have considered and may not want to consider. I don't think of these questions as Humble Inquiry because asking for feelings may be pushing deeper than the other is willing to go. Asking about feelings is one way to personalize the relationship, which may or may not be appropriate in the situation you are in at that moment.

**2) Causes and Motives**—questions about motivation or about causes that focus the others on their motivations in relation to something that they have been talking about

Examples:

"Why did that happen?"

"Why did (do) you feel that way?"

"What may have caused this . . . ?"

"Why do you suppose that happened?"

With such questions I am clearly forcing the other person to join me in figuring out what may be going on and am satisfying my curiosity. Whether or not we view this as

Humble Inquiry depends upon how relevant the inquiry and the answer are to accomplishing our common task.

**3) Action Oriented**—questions that focus others on what they did, are thinking about doing, or plan to do in the future

If others have already reported actions, I can build on that. But often when people present their problems, they don't reveal past, present, or possible future actions, which I might need to bring out with questions.

Examples:

"What have you tried so far?"

"How did you get here?"

"What did you (he/she/they) *do* about that?" (in response to a complaint)

"What are you going to *do* next?"

Action-oriented questions clearly push the other person even further into your line of thinking. In that sense, these questions also influence the other's mental process and should be used only when you feel justified in exerting that influence. For example, in the case of the COO whose leadership team always sat in the same seats, I bluntly asked him, "What did you *do*?" I felt this was justified because we were both trying to solve the problem of understanding the culture he was in. My steering him into thinking about his actions was legitimated by the fact that I was in the helper role and we were working on a joint task.

**4) Systemic Questions**—questions that build understanding of the total situation

Stories that others tell us about themselves typically involve other people as well—family members, friends, bosses, colleagues, and/or subordinates. You may decide that it is important for you and the teller to understand the reactions or actions of others that have been mentioned and may, therefore, ask what someone else in the other's social system might be thinking, feeling, or doing. This form of questioning is very powerful if you and the other have agreed to explore a situation in greater detail.

Examples:

"What did she (he/they) *do* then?"

"How do you think she felt when you did that?"

"What do you think he will do if you follow through on what you said?"

"How would they have reacted if you had told them how you felt?"

These four kinds of diagnostic questions steer one's mental process and help one to become more self-aware. However, they are still questions and they do not imply any particular solution. They may qualify as Humble Inquiry depending on the context in which they are asked and the state of the relationship.

## CONFRONTATIONAL INQUIRY

The essence of confrontational inquiry is that you now insert your *own ideas* but in the form of a question. When we talk about rhetorical questions or leading questions, we are acknowledging that the question is really a form of telling. The question may still be based on curiosity or interest, but it is now in connection to your own interests. I now want information related to something that I want to do or am thinking about.

Almost by definition this form of inquiry can rarely qualify as Humble Inquiry because the inquirer is taking charge of both the process and content of the conversation. You are tacitly giving advice, and this often arouses resistance in others and makes it harder to build relationships with them because they have to explain or defend why they aren't feeling something or doing something that you proposed.

Confrontational questions can cover the same categories of diagnosis as above.

1) **Feelings and Reactions**

"Did that not make you angry?"

vs.

"How did that make you feel?"

2) **Causes and Motives**

"Do you think they were sitting that way because they were scared?"

vs.

"Why do you suppose they were sitting that way?"

3) **Action Oriented**

"Why didn't you say something to the group?"

vs.

"What did you do?"

"Why don't we go to the movies tonight?"

vs.

"What shall we do tonight?"

"Have you thought of going on a diet?"

vs.

"What are you doing about your weight?

4) **Systemic Questions**

"Were the others in the room surprised?"

vs.

"How were the others in the room reacting?"

Confrontational questions can be humble if your motive is to be helpful and if the relationship has enough trust built up to allow the other to feel helped rather than confronted. Timing, tone of voice, and various other cues tell the listener about your motives. What I have found most important is to ask myself what my motives are before I ask a confrontational question. Am I feeling humble and curious or have I fallen into thinking I have an answer and am just testing out whether or not I am right? If I am just testing my own thought, then I have drifted into telling and should not be surprised if the other person gets defensive. When I asked "What did you *do?*" of the COO whose team sat in the same spots, I clearly had no thought in my head as to what he might have done. But our culture of Tell is so strong that when I relate this story to fellow consultants and ask them what they would have said if they had been in my shoes, most of them come up with various suggestions to the COO instead of the open question I asked.

## PROCESS-ORIENTED INQUIRY

An option that is always on the table is to shift the conversational focus onto the conversation itself. Whether this counts as Humble Inquiry or not depends on the motives of the person shifting the focus. If I am trying to develop a good relationship and feel the conversation going in the wrong direction, I can humbly ask some version of "What is happening?" ("Are we OK?" "Did I offend you?") to explore what might be wrong and how it might be fixed. Instead of continuing with the content of the conversation, this kind of inquiry suddenly focuses on the here-and-now interaction. Just how this might be worded depends very much on the actual situation, but it would always make the other person conscious that there is a two-person interaction going on and that it can be reviewed and analyzed.

Process-oriented inquiry can also be categorized.

1) **Humble Process Inquiry**

   "What is happening here?"

   "Have we gone too far?"

   "Is this too personal?"

2) **Diagnostic Process Inquiry**

   "Why did you choose to tell me about your feelings in this particular way?"

   "What do you think is happening between us right now?"

   "What should I be asking you now?"

3) **Confrontational Process Inquiry**

   "Why were you so defensive just now when I was trying to tell you how I felt?"

   "Are you upset, have I upset you?"

   "Are you stimulated by what I am asking you?"

The power of this kind of inquiry is that it focuses on the relationship itself and enables both parties to assess whether their relationship goals are being met. Used with humility this kind of inquiry is probably also the most difficult to learn because our culture does not support it as normal conversation. Except in special training events we tend to avoid talking about *how* we are talking or saying something specific about our relationship. Yet this form of inquiry is often the most powerful way to get out of awkward or difficult conversations because it allows both parties to reset, to restate what they are there for, what they want, and, in other ways, recalibrate their expectations.

## In Summary

Saying to oneself that one should *ask* more and *tell* less does not solve the problem of building a relationship of mutual trust. The underlying attitude of competitive one-upmanship will leak out if it is there. Humble Inquiry starts with the attitude and is then supported by our choice of questions. The more we remain curious about the other person rather than letting our own expectations and preconceptions creep in, the better our chances are of staying in the right questioning mode. We have to learn that diagnostic and confrontational questions come very naturally and easily, just as telling comes naturally and easily. It takes some discipline and practice to access one's ignorance, to stay focused on the other person.

If we learn to do this, the positive consequences will be better conversations and better relationships. For many situations it may not matter; we may not care. But especially if you are dependent on others—if you are the boss or senior person trying to increase the likelihood that your subordinates will help you and be open with you—then Humble Inquiry will not only be desirable but essential.

Why is this so difficult? We need next to look at the cultural forces that favor telling.

**QUESTIONS FOR THE READER**

- Think about a recent conversation you have had and see if you can classify the questions that you asked and that the other person asked into the four categories of question types.

- Do the same thing for a recent interview that you conducted. Do you detect any biases in the choice of questions that you asked?

- Think about a time that you were interviewed. What questions were asked? How did you react to them? Were some easier to deal with than others? Did some draw you out more than others? Which ones?

- What conclusions can you draw about yourself as an asker and teller, based on your answers to the above three questions?

- Now take a few minutes just to reflect quietly on what you have learned in general so far.

# 4

# The Culture of Do and Tell

The main inhibitor of Humble Inquiry is the culture in which we grew up. Culture can be thought of as manifesting itself on many levels—it is represented by all of its artifacts, by which I mean buildings, art works, products, language, and everything that we see and feel when we enter another culture.[5] But artifacts are not easy to decipher, so when we enter a new culture we find that we have to talk to people and ask them questions about what things mean. When we do that, we elicit the level of culture that I call *espoused values* such as freedom, equality of opportunity, individual rights, and other values that are often referred to as "our constitutional rights."

When we compare some of the artifacts and behaviors that we observe with some of the values that we are told about, we find inconsistencies, which tell us that there is a deeper level to culture, one that includes what we can think of as tacit *assumptions*. Such assumptions may have been values at one time, but, by consensus, they have come to be taken for granted and dropped out of conscious debate. It is these assumptions that really drive the manifest behavioral elements and are, therefore, the essence of a culture.

The most common example of this in the United States is that we claim to value teamwork and talk about it all the time, but the artifacts—our promotional systems and rewards systems—are entirely individualistic. We espouse equality of opportunity and freedom, but the artifacts—poorer education, little opportunity, and various forms of discrimination for ghetto minorities—suggest that there are other assumptions having to do with pragmatism and "rugged individualism" that operate all the time and really determine our behavior.

The tacit assumptions that make up a given culture may or may not be congruent with each other. Cultures can exist with inconsistencies and internal conflict. With respect to a particular set of behaviors, such as humility, it is important to identify the relevant cultural assumptions and assess their impact. We especially need to understand the tacit assumptions around authority, relationships, and trust.

All cultures have rules about status and respect based on deep assumptions about what merits status. In many societies basic humility toward persons whose positions are based on birthright is taken for granted and automatically felt. In societies that are Western, more egalitarian, and individualistic, we tend to respect only high achievers, based on the Horatio Alger myth of working one's way up from the bottom. We tend to experience *optional humility* in the presence of those who have achieved more, but the Here-and-now Humility, based on awareness of dependency, is often missing.

The degree to which superiors and subordinates can be humble differs by the basic assumptions of the culture they grew up in. The more authoritarian the culture, the greater the sociological distance between the upper and lower levels of status or achievement, and, therefore, the harder it is for the superior to be humble and learn the art of Humble Inquiry. Beyond these general points about culture, why do specific aspects of the U.S. culture make Humble Inquiry more difficult?

## THE MAIN PROBLEM—A CULTURE THAT VALUES TASK ACCOMPLISHMENT MORE THAN RELATIONSHIP BUILDING

The U.S. culture is individualistic, competitive, optimistic, and pragmatic. We believe that the basic unit of society is the individual, whose rights have to be protected at all costs. We are entrepreneurial and admire individual accomplishment. We thrive on competition. Optimism and pragmatism show up in the way we are oriented toward the short term and in our dislike of long-range planning. We do not like to fix things and improve them while they are still working. We prefer to run things until they break because we believe we can then fix them or replace them. We are arrogant and deep down believe we can fix anything—"The impossible just takes a little longer." We are impatient and, with information technology's ability to do things faster, we are even more impatient. Most important of all, *we value task accomplishment over relationship building* and either are not aware of this cultural bias or, worse, *don't care and don't want to be bothered with it.*

We do not like or trust groups. We believe that committees and meetings are a waste of time and that group decisions diffuse accountability. We only spend money and time on team building when it appears to be pragmatically necessary to get the job done. We tout and admire teamwork and the winning team (espoused values), but we don't for a minute believe that the team could have done it without the individual star, who usually receives much greater pay (tacit assumption).

We would never consider for a moment paying the team members equally. In the Olympics we usually have some of the world's fastest runners yet have lost some of the relay races because we could not pass the baton without dropping

it! We take it for granted that accountability must be individual; there must be someone to praise for victory and someone
to blame for defeat, the individual where "the buck stops."

In fact, instead of admiring relationships, we value and
admire individual competitiveness, winning out over each
other, outdoing each other conversationally, pulling the
clever con game, and selling stuff that the customer does
not need. We believe in *caveat emptor* (let the buyer beware),
and we justify exploitation with "There's a sucker born every
minute." We breed mistrust of strangers, but we don't have
any formulas for how to test or build trust. We value our freedom without realizing that this breeds caution and mistrust
of each other. When we are taken in by a Ponzi scheme and
lose all our money, we don't blame our culture or our own
greed—we blame the regulators who should have caught it
and kick ourselves for not getting in on it earlier.

In politics we build relationships with some people to
further our goals and in order to gain advantage over other
people. We build coalitions in order to gain power and, in
that process, make it more necessary to be careful in deciding whom we can trust. We assume that we can automatically trust family only to discover betrayal among family
members. Basically, in our money-conscious society of
today, we don't really know whom to trust and, worse, we
don't know how to create a trusting relationship. We value
loyalty in the abstract, but in our pluralistic society, it is not
at all clear to whom one should be loyal beyond oneself.

When we deal with people in other cultures that consider relationships to be intrinsic to getting the job done by
building trust first, we get impatient with spending time over
relationship-building dinners before getting down to work.
When we are sent off to outward-bound retreats to build
teamwork, we view that as a necessary price of doing busi-

ness and sometimes even enjoy and benefit but still think of it as just a means to the end of task accomplishment.

When the airlines first investigated some of their serious accidents, they found that some resulted from communication failures in the cockpit. In several dramatic cases the senior person just plain did not pay attention to the junior person who was giving out key information as the plane crashed. For a time, the airlines launched team-training programs and even assigned crews that had trained together to work with each other in the cockpit. But when this became too expensive and too unwieldy to manage, they went back to a rotational system where checklists and professionalism were expected to facilitate the necessary communication. It was even reported that some teams became overconfident and developed bad habits leading to safety shortcuts that justified dropping the team training.

In the United States, status and prestige are gained by task accomplishment, and once you are above someone else, you are licensed to tell them what to do. The best engineer and the best salesperson are promoted to be supervisors where they can now tell others what to do. Social distance across rank levels is considered OK. In fact, personal relationships across ranks are considered dangerous because they could lead to bias in assigning work and rewards. In the military, if the officer had a personal relationship with a subordinate, it would make it more difficult to decide whom to send on a potentially lethal mission. Officers shouldn't fraternize with the troops.

In medicine today, we vocally deplore the fact that the system limits the amount of time that doctors can spend with patients because of our espoused value that building a relationship with patients is good medicine, but we accept short visits as an inevitable pragmatic necessity because of the tacit assumption that economic criteria rather than social ones should drive the system. We accept what we regard as economic necessities even though there is growing evidence that communication problems between doctors and patients cause treatment failures and are sometimes responsible for patients taking the wrong doses of a medicine. Valuing task accomplishment over relationship building shows up in how often doctors are disrespectful of nurses and technicians and even of patients. They often depersonalize and ignore the patient in their discussion with the interns who have been brought along to view the "case." All of this is driven by the need to accomplish tasks in a cost-effective manner, which translates into cramming as many tasks as possible into each unit of time and not bothering with relationship building because that might take too long.

This may seem like a harsh view of our culture, and there are certainly trends in other directions, but when we deal with culture at the tacit assumption level we have to think clearly about what our assumptions actually are, quite apart from our espoused values. The result of a pragmatic, individualistic, competitive, task-oriented culture is that humility is low on the value scale.

## A SECOND PROBLEM—THE CULTURE OF TELL

We take it for granted that telling is more valued than asking. Asking the *right* questions is valued, but asking in general is not. To ask is to reveal ignorance and weakness. Knowing things is highly valued, and telling people what we know is almost automatic because we have made it habitual in most situations. We are especially prone to telling when we have been empowered by someone else's question or when we have been formally promoted into a position of power. I once asked a group of management students what it meant to them to be promoted to "manager." They said without hesitation, "It means I can now tell others what to do." Of course, the dangerous and hidden assumption in that dictum is that once people are promoted that they will then know what to do. The idea that the manager might come to a subordinate and ask, "What should we do?" would be considered abdication, failure to fulfill your role. If you are a manager or a leader, you are supposed to know what to do, or at least appear to know.

Knowing things is highly valued in most cultures. With age we supposedly get wiser, which usually means knowing more. So we go to older people to get answers and expect to get them. When the supplicant climbs the mountain to reach the wise guru, and his question is answered with another question, we put this into a cartoon and laugh about it. Telling is not only expected and respected, but it feels so good when we think we have solved someone else's problem. What is more satisfying than giving advice?

We still live in a culture of what Stephen Potter so eloquently described in the 1950s as *gamesmanship* and *one-upmanship*.[6] These were the two titles that best characterized what Potter saw to be the main characteristic of relationships in the Western world. It was British humor at its best, but it was a much deeper commentary on how Western culture values competition, even in conversation. Potter notes that there are several ways to gain points in competitive conversation: making a smart remark, putting down someone who has claimed too much, and turning a clever phrase even if it embarrasses someone else in the conversation. We compete on who can tell the *most*—the most interesting story, the most outrageous adventure, the best joke, or the best movie they saw.

Of course, outdoing someone else is only good if it is

done within the cultural rules of etiquette. Embarrassing or humiliating someone in the conversation is not good and, if one consistently does this, one gets socially ostracized, or, if it is extreme, one gets put into a mental hospital. To be an effective *gamesman* or *lifeman*, Potter notes, one must know "how to win without *actually* cheating" or practice "the art of getting away with it without being an absolute plonk." In presidential pre-election debates we only care who won and often base that decision not on who did the best analysis of the issues but who looked most presidential in front of the cameras and who turned the best phrase or made the most clever put-down.

One possible implication in all of this is that deep down many of us believe that if you are not winning, you are losing. If you don't tell first, someone else will tell and get the brownie points. The tacit assumption based on our biological roots is that life is fundamentally and always a competition. Someone has to be the alpha male. The idea of reciprocal *cooperation* where *both parties win* is not on our radar screen except where pragmatically necessary or in special events such as improvisation theater where each person's job is to set up his partner to deliver the good line that gets the laughs. That requires the building of a relationship in which one-upmanship is not desirable.

We also know how important telling is from our desire in most conversations to get to the point. When we are listening to someone and don't see where it is going, we say, "So what is your point?" We expect conversations to reach some kind of conclusion, which is reached by telling something, not by asking questions. When we are in the telling mode, we hope to educate, to impress, to score points, to entertain; when we are in the listening mode, we want to be educated, impressed, and entertained.

When we listen, we want to feel that it was *worthwhile* to listen. It is frustrating to have someone tell us something that we cannot use or that is boring. My worst occasions of this sort are when someone tells stories about people whom I don't know in situations that I have never experienced. In other words, we don't want to be told any old things. What we want to be told and what we choose to tell have to be useful—they need to be in context and they need to be relevant.

Finally, nothing is more frustrating to listeners than to be told things or given advice that they already know and/ or have already thought of and dismissed as impractical. It makes you feel demeaned when you realize that the teller thinks you have not already thought of this yourself. But, paradoxically, telling is so ingrained that we don't think about this issue when we are about to tell someone something. Before we give advice, do we really consider whether or not the person to whom we are telling this might have already thought of it? I suspect that we all do much more telling than we should.

## Why Is This Important Now?
## The Changing Demands of Future Tasks

There is, of course, much more to U.S. culture than what I have described. And things are changing. The assumptions I described may be less relevant to the next couple of generations. The recognition of interdependency is growing with the growth of information technology. So why focus on these particular biases in our culture? Consider again the operating room of today in which the surgeon, the anesthesiologist, key nursing staff, and surgical technicians have to work in perfect harmony with each other in undertaking a complex operation. Consider that they not only have different professions and ranks, but they are likely to be of different generations and possibly different national cultures, which may have their own values and norms around relationships, authority, and trust. So let me restate the problem:

> **The world is becoming more technologically complex, interdependent, and culturally diverse, which makes the building of relationships more and more necessary to get things accomplished and, at the same time, more difficult. Relationships are the key to good communication; good communication is the key to successful task accomplishment; and Humble Inquiry, based on Here-and-now Humility, is the key to good relationships.**

Increasingly, tasks resemble kids on a seesaw or a relay team. Coaches of American football often point out that *every* position has to do its job or the play fails. A chorus has to practice together so that *every* member will be able to deal with all the musical variations that different conductors may want from it. A surgical team requires perfect coordination from *every* member. Producing a successful webcast requires perfect coordination among the senders and receivers. Flying an airliner safely requires perfect coordination from the entire crew, as do all kinds of processes in the chemical and nuclear industries. All of these group situations require the members of the group to build relationships with each other that go beyond just "professionals working with each other." Checklists and other formal processes of coordination are not enough because they cannot deal with unanticipated situations. Through Humble Inquiry teams can build the initial relationships that enable them to learn together. As they build higher levels of trust through joint learning, they become more open in their communication, which, in turn, enables them to deal with the inevitable surprises that arise in complex interdependent situations.[7]

The irony is that when we see good task accomplishment that results from relationships and higher levels of trust, we admire it and almost treat it as a surprising anomaly, thereby admitting tacitly that it is culturally not *normal*. In the world of professional football, when a team acquires a player who knows either some of the present players or the coach from having been on another team together, the team as a whole may improve because there is already a clearly built relationship that enables them to play better with each other.

In other words, we know intuitively and from experience that we work better in a complex interdependent task with someone we know and trust, but we are not prepared to spend the effort, time, and money to ensure that such relationships are built. We value such relationships when they are built as part of the work itself, as in military operations where soldiers form intense personal relationships with their buddies. We admire the loyalty to each other and the heroism that is displayed on behalf of someone with whom one has a relationship, but when we see such deep relationships in a business organization, we consider it unusual. And programs for team building are often the first things cut in the budget when cost issues arise.

## The Special Challenge to Leaders

Culturally it is more appropriate for the person of higher status to do more telling and for the subordinate to do more inquiring and listening. This works when 1) both parties have the same superordinate goal, 2) the superior knows the answers, and 3) the subordinate understands what is being told. Superiors need to find out whether those three conditions are met in a particular situation. To return to our relay race analogy, the leader has to find out whether all four members want to win, whether the baton passers (bosses or subordinates) know how to communicate to the receivers how the baton will be passed, and whether instructions such as "pick up speed when I enter the zone" are, in fact, clear enough to be understood.

If bosses don't build relationships with their subordinates through initial Humble Inquiry, they will not be able to tell whether or not communication is good, because in many situations the subordinates will not admit that they don't understand or they may withhold critical safety information because they do not share the superordinate goal. Or the boss may announce the superordinate goal of safety but be unwittingly sending signals that cost and speed are just as important. If surgeons have not built relationships with their teams, team members may withhold information and jeopardize patient safety because they do not feel psychologically safe to speak up to the higher-status person.

The more complex the task, the greater the degree of interdependence and the more the boss has to acknowledge a Here-and-now Humility and engage in Humble Inquiry. Yet remember that it is primarily an attitude, that there is no formula for exactly how to do it. Sensing and feeling inevitably come into play in deciding what is the current state of the relationship and what is the situation. However, the demeanor of the higher-status person should always be to build status, to give face. Only by making the subordinate feel psychologically safe can the superior hope to get the information and help needed. If they share the same superordinate goals, such as winning the relay race, keeping patients safe, and keeping the nuclear plant from having an accident, that will help but never be enough. Subordinates are always in a vulnerable position and must, therefore, first be reassured before they will fully commit to open communication and collaboration.

Consider again the situation of the hospital patient. One thing that the doctor can offer in this situation by humbly inquiring is to make the patient feel like a whole person rather than a scientific subject. The oncologist who asked my wife about our travel plans won her over immediately because she realized he cared about us, not just about containing the cancer. Consider the leader in the relay race who asks whether the receiver is right- or left-handed and has a preference or a need that should be considered. Consider the surgeon who says to the team, "I am completely dependent on you. What do we need to work out to make things go smoothly?" Consider the lawyer who has taken over the power company site that contains a nuclear plant and goes to the operators and maintenance people to ask what they do, what their world is like, what worries them. Such Humble Inquiry becomes especially relevant when leaders realize they are completely dependent on all the workers in the plant doing their jobs, using a technology that they themselves do not understand and, therefore, could not tell the workers what to do even if they wanted to. Consider how much of the work done in today's technologically complex world cannot be done by the leader; hence the leader must learn to live with Here-and-now Humility. Now that the particular problems of asking and telling in superior-subordinate relationships have been identified, the next chapter explores further the impacts of culture, rank, and status and suggests how they can best be approached.

## In Summary

The U.S. culture is strongly built on the tacit assumptions of pragmatism, individualism, and status through achievement. These assumptions introduce a strong bias for getting the job done, which, combined with individualism, leads to a devaluing of relationship building, teamwork, and collaboration except as means to the end of task accomplishment. Given those cultural biases, doing and telling are inevitably valued more than asking and relationship building. However, as tasks become more complex and interdependent, collaboration, teamwork, and relationship building will become more necessary. That, in turn, will require leaders to become more skilled in Humble Inquiry.

**QUESTIONS FOR THE READER**

- Think back to the last party you attended. What kind of talk was going on? Can you think of examples of competitive telling? Can you think of examples of relationship building? What was the difference in the quality of the talk?

- Can you think of examples in your work setting that illustrate the impact of cultural characteristics on task performance and communication?

- In your work setting, what examples come to mind of *doing* being more highly valued than *relationship building*? What instances can you recall when *telling* trumped *asking* questions?

- Think about your family situation. Do you have family dinners or other kinds of regular get-togethers? What is the quality of the talk at those times?

- Now take a few minutes just to reflect quietly on what you have learned in general so far.

# 5

## Status, Rank, and Role Boundaries as Inhibitors

How we relate to another person, whether we tell or ask, whether we want to build more trust and openness, whether we just want acknowledgment or something more, is best thought of in terms of *situations*. In every culture children are taught how to behave and feel in a variety of situations. These situations are defined by the mutual intentions of the people coming together and, within a given culture, most of us know what is situationally appropriate—the rules and the etiquette governing the situation. Most of us are so thoroughly acculturated that we are unaware of these rules and how scripted we are. This is true especially in situations in which the participants are of different rank or status.

### Status and Rank

In order to understand some of the inhibitors of Humble Inquiry, we have to examine particularly the rules pertaining to behavior between people of different status or rank. From the subordinates' points of view, these rules can best be thought of as the rules of *deference*, or how subordinates are supposed to show respect for their superiors; from the superiors' points of view, they are the rules of *demeanor*, or how superiors are supposed to act in a way that is appropriate to their status. For example, when the superior is speaking, the subordinate is supposed to pay attention and not interrupt; the superior is supposed to make sense and behave in a dignified manner.

We take these rules so for granted that we only notice them when they are situationally inappropriate, as when a subordinate speaks out of turn or a leader says or does something that is insulting or stupid. We have very clear expectations about what is the appropriate demeanor for a high-status person, and it arouses anxiety and anger when those expectations are not met. It is not accidental that higher-status people are given private bathrooms so that they can properly compose themselves before appearing in public.

Similarly, we have clear rules about deference, which vary depending on the culture. A dramatic case of misunderstanding such rules occurred years ago in the South African gold mines when white supervisors consistently viewed tribal workers as being untrustworthy because they were "shifty eyed" and "never looked you in the eye." It took years of supervisory training to teach the white managers that in the tribal culture looking a superior in the eye was a mark of *disrespect* and would be punished.

When we enter a new situation or meet someone and start a conversation, one of the first things that we sort out unconsciously is the relative status distinctions that must be observed. Some might argue we are still biologically programmed to locate ourselves in the pecking order. We often start with Humble Inquiry in such a situation because it provides an opportunity to find out whether the other person in the conversation is of higher or lower status, whether we should be deferent or alternatively should expect deference. We start by asking general questions—what kind of work do you do? Where do you live? What brings you here? If the cues are that the other person is of lower status, as when some undergraduates approached me at a recent meeting and asked to have their picture taken with me because they had read and liked some of my work, I automatically assumed the appropriate demeanor of being flattered and posed urbanely with a big smile. On the other hand, this same kind of instant adjustment was illustrated when I was recently introduced to a fellow resident of my retirement complex and learned that he was a Nobel Prize–winning physicist. I found myself feeling humble and asking very open-ended questions to learn more about him. Since we were of similar age and both residents in the same retirement community, he also took a more humble position well into the conversation, which reduced the status gap and led to a more informal open exchange.

In summary, situational rules determine the appropriate form of Humble Inquiry where there is a status or rank difference at the outset of the conversation. What we have to learn as we look ahead to more interdependent tasks is how to bridge those status gaps when we are in fact mutually dependent on each other. It will be easy for the subordinate to continue to be humble and ask for the help of the superior. The dilemma that will require new learning is how the superior can learn to ask for help from the subordinate. To begin to understand how to deal with that dilemma, we have to look also at different types of role relations.

## TYPES OF ROLE RELATIONS—
## TASK ORIENTED AND PERSONAL ORIENTED

One determinant that defines the rules of a situation is relative status. Equally important in defining the situation is the role relationship of the parties or the purpose for which they have gotten together. Am I meeting a friend for lunch, approaching a salesperson to buy new shoes, visiting my doctor, or being introduced to my new boss (or subordinate)? My purpose defines the task and the kind of situation I want to create. When I then come together with others, we jointly define the situation—what is it we are here to do, what is our role in the situation, what do we expect of each other, and what kind of relationship is this to be?

Sociologists have proposed various ways to classify all the kinds of relationships that we get into. To understand Humble Inquiry, it is useful to distinguish particularly between *instrumental* relationships, in which one person needs something specific from the other person, and *expressive* relationships, which are driven by personal needs to build the relationship because one or both of the people involved are beginning to like the other. To simplify, I will call these task-oriented and person-oriented relationships. As I argued in the last chapter, U.S. culture is much more concerned with task-oriented relationships—getting together to get the job done. These relationships often are labeled "professional," which implies working together competently but avoiding personal involvement. Getting personal is often viewed as "unprofessional."

We think of task-oriented relationships as impersonal and emotionally neutral. Relative status is defined by the degree of dependence, which defines the degree of Here-and-now Humility that is appropriate. When I am buying a suit, the salesman is dependent on my decision and will be very deferent and humble. When I have bought it, and the tailor is measuring me for alterations, he tells me how to stand, and I become very Here-and-now Humble. We both know the culturally defined situational rules and try to stay as emotionally uninvolved as possible. When we deal with a salesperson, we expect a certain amount of emotional distance, conversation limited to the product, price, and delivery issues. We develop mutual respect based on the particular knowledge and skill that the salesperson has.

By contrast, a person-oriented relationship is expected to be more emotionally charged because one or both parties are interested in each other and expect or want the relationship to continue. This kind of relationship allows for, even expects, some emotional expression. When we want to get to know someone better, we are moving into a personal relationship. When we want our subordinates to maintain a respectful distance, we are defining the situation as task-oriented. As I mentioned before, one is not expected to fraternize with the troops.

For both types of relationships we carry within us cultural rules about what is and is not appropriate. The reason we are not supposed to interrupt the boss is that the boss-subordinate relationship is, in most organizations, defined as task driven with the hierarchy defining degrees and types of task competence. If the boss plays golf with the janitor, we raise our eyebrows and wonder what the implications are of this unusual relationship. In our surgical team described above, the rules at the outset are very clear about the status hierarchy and that each relationship in the team is instrumental, impersonal, and emotionally neutral. In other words, task interdependence requires Here-and-now Humility but does not in principle have to become personal or emotionally charged.

A huge question is whether with growing task complexity and cultural diversity it will be possible to maintain these status boundaries. Or will relationship building in the task arena inevitably require some degree of personalization?

We don't notice these rules and boundaries until they

are violated, as when parties in a task-oriented relationship do become emotionally involved. We can accept the boss having an affair outside the organization, but we become very punitive if the affair is with a subordinate or co-worker because it implies that special favors will be granted or, worse, that task performance will be compromised because incompetence might be tolerated.

As we think about our various relationships, they are, of course, not cleanly divisible into task oriented and personal. We develop feelings and liking for people with whom we have strict task-oriented relationships, and we find that sometimes our friends and lovers become crucial to some task accomplishment. However, when the rules are violated or ambiguous, as when different cultures are involved, relationships can be damaged. An extreme case I heard about recently involved a house owner with a Filipino maid. The owner liked the maid and wanted to personalize the relationship only to be rebuffed repeatedly. The maid quit, and the owner found out, through the maid of a mutual friend, that in the culture from which the maid came, it was totally inappropriate to hold any kind of personal conversation with the person employing you.

So, for our purposes, it is most useful to think of a *continuum* that stretches from the extremely task oriented to the extremely personal. The question we must then ask is whether the key to making interdependent relationships work is to *personalize them to some degree*. And, if so, how can Humble Inquiry make that happen?

## PERSONALIZATION AS RELATIONSHIP BUILDING

Personalization is the process of acknowledging the other person as a whole human, not just a role. The minimal level of personalization in this sense would be to share first and last names. So when Dr. Brown is first introduced to his operating room nurse as Ms. Grant and his anesthetist as Dr. Tanaka, this would be an example of formal role introductions. In a formal traditional hospital setting, that is what would be done, and that would be the end of it. If the hospital head wanted to personalize the relationship somewhat, the initial introduction by the chief of surgery might be "Dr. Brown, this will be your nurse, *Amy* Grant, and your anesthetist, Dr. *Yoshi* Tanaka." Such minimal personalization might have powerful effects if it is a change from past practice. And it may possibly bend the rules a bit as well, if the hospital tradition has been one of maintaining professional decorum. I know of one hospital that decided on first names among the medical staff but *never in front of patients* because the patient had to be reminded of the relative statuses of the medical team members. Would the patient lose respect for Dr. Brown if Amy called him "Rod?"

Once the process of personalization has been launched and accepted, in that both parties display comfort with first names, the Pandora's box is opened to endless other personal questions and revelations. But this process is not without its own situational propriety that we all live by. Staying on the role/task level, Dr. Brown might ask Amy where she got her training, what other doctors she had worked with, whether she was headed for a particular specialty, and so on. If he wanted to become more personal, he might ask some questions about where she lives, whether she has a family, where she is from, and what she thinks of the hospital in which they both work. The question about her view of the hospital might be pushing the boundary in that she might not know how safe it would be to tell Dr. Brown exactly what she thought and felt, especially if she had some criticisms.

How personalization might proceed from this point

on might depend very much on when and where this conversation was being held. Amy Edmondson, in her study of cardiac surgical teams doing open-heart surgery, reported that some of these teams functioned better in doing this very complicated surgery than others.[8] At a recent meeting, she mentioned a detail that is central to this analysis. Edmondson was in the cafeteria where all the staff tended to sit by rank and occupation, and she noticed that one of these successful teams was sitting at a table *with each other.* Evidently they had decided that spending time with each other was more important than for each of them to eat with their professional peers. This decision enabled them to explore getting to know each other at a more personal level, something that they evidently felt they needed to do in order to function well as a team in the OR. Edmondson's study showed that the teams that were able to adopt and successfully utilize the more complex surgical process had made a special effort to learn together as a team and, thereby, reduce status differences and make everyone aware of their mutual interdependence. Eating together was just one of many activities that personalized their relationships.

The point is that a small change—whom one eats lunch with—has huge symbolic implications for relationship building in that the senior doctor is publicly humbling himself by sitting with his subordinate staff, thereby empowering them to be more open with him.

In another example, one of Edmondson's doctoral students, Melissa Valentine, studied hospital emergency rooms that were overloaded and needed to find a solution to the long times that patients spent in the emergency unit.[9] One hospital decided to create small "pods" consisting of one of every kind of intake professional needed to treat emergency cases. Patients and staff would be arbitrarily assigned to pods based on where there was a vacancy at that moment. What this meant was that, over a period of time, each doctor, nurse, and technician would meet many other doctors, nurses, and technicians but always in a small-group context that facilitated personalization. Instead of a nurse having to find a doctor when a patient was ready to be seen, there was always a doctor available in the pod. The smaller size of the pod created more opportunities for face-to-face interaction, which made Humble Inquiry and personalization easier.

Humble Inquiry is by definition more personal because it hinges on being curious about and interested in the other person, but the choice of topic can range from task related to very intimate. That choice also has to take into account various cultural factors because what is considered personal is itself determined by rules that derive from organizational histories, the cultures of occupations, and national cultures.

## Organizational, Occupational, and National Culture

Situational proprieties are influenced by the history of relationships in the particular organization in which the tasks are to be accomplished. Organizations and occupations with a history do develop their own traditions and rules within the traditions and rules of the larger society. Within the organization there will be occupational units with their own cultural rules about deference and demeanor. Among scientists and engineers there tends to be much more open communication and mutual respect based on what people know and can do. Even within occupations such as engineering, there will be different rules—electrical engineers work with a here-and-now technology that lends itself to experimentation and frequent open communication; chemical engineering is much more formal and hierarchic because chemistry does not easily lend itself to casual experimentation.

In medicine there are occupational traditions among doctors and nurses, which create professional distance. A structural intervention, such as changing the size and composition of units in the emergency room, might be a seemingly sensible change to implement for more personalization to occur, but if the hospital's culture is firmly anchored in a very strong tradition of professional distance, the members of this hospital would find the pod system uncomfortable and unworkable. In other words, the situational proprieties defined by the culture of the organization and the occupations might well override efforts by some members of the team to attempt to personalize relationships. Amy might have come from a personalized system, and when she suggests to Drs. Brown and Tanaka that they might all have lunch together, she might find herself firmly rebuffed. In fact, Melissa Valentine reported that in her research she encountered hospitals that refused the pod system because it would force more closeness than that staff was ready for.[10]

The nuclear industry provides an interesting example of occupational culture because most of the officers and plant managers who populated the industry for the first few decades were products of the nuclear submarine fleet that had a very strong culture based an Admiral Rickover's absolute concern for safety. As they retired and new managers came in with different backgrounds, communication problems arose. The absolute respect that the old managers had for safety based on their intimate knowledge of the technology was sometimes not shared by the new plant managers who came from law or finance.

I have focused this analysis on the United States and Western culture, but the example of Dr. Brown and his team reminds us that different nationalities and ethnic groups are increasingly involved in the various kinds of tasks performed. How to be humble and how to explore more personal issues in order to build a positive relationship becomes even more important and difficult if we don't know the norms of other cultures. For example, I know of one surgical team that consists of a U.S. surgeon, a Muslim nurse from Tunisia, a Muslim Tech, and a Latino anesthetist. When I interviewed this doctor, he not only admitted from the outset that "he was completely dependent on them," but then told me of the many ways he had worked on getting to know them and spent time informally with them. Now he feels that they are completely at ease with each other, and he trusts them to be totally open with him. Knowing about these other cultures in the abstract did not help, but systematically personalizing his relationship to his team members did.

## Trust and Social Economics

To be humble, to ask instead of telling, to try to personalize the relationship to some degree requires some level of trust, yet *trust* is one of those words that we all think we know the meaning of but is very hard to define. Trust in the context of a conversation is believing that the other person will acknowledge me, not take advantage of me, not embarrass or humiliate me, tell me the truth, and, in the broader context, not cheat me, work on my behalf, and support the goals we have agreed to.

The importance of basic acknowledgment can be seen in our daily routines in terms of whom we look at, bow our head to, and speak to. If I pass a stranger on the street and make eye contact, and then we both go on without further expression, that feels normal because we don't expect acknowledgment. But if I see someone I know, we make eye contact, I smile, and the other person shows no sign of recognition, I feel that something is amiss. I have not been recognized or acknowledged. Why not? What is wrong? It is this feeling of something being amiss that reminds us how much we count on mutual recognition and reciprocation. We may not remember someone's name, but our greeting and our demeanor tells the other person that we acknowledge them. Becoming socially invisible can become traumatic.

Society is based on a minimum amount of this kind of taken-for-granted trust. We trust that we will be acknowledged as fellow humans and that our presented self will be affirmed. It is taken for granted in the sense that when we say hello to someone with an actual greeting or just nod of the head, we expect a response of some kind. If we ask a question, we expect some kind of an answer. If we ask for help, we expect either to be helped or to be offered an excuse as to why we cannot be helped. If we ask others to do something, we expect them to do it or to offer a reason why they cannot.

Life in civilized society is reciprocal, and we all learn the rules of the culture in which we grow up of when and how to reciprocate. We think of those behaviors as good manners, etiquette, and tact, and sometimes forget that it is not optional—it is the very basis of society.

Basic trust is learned and constantly tested as we grow up in civilized society. The basic rules will vary from culture to culture, but every culture will have such rules. As adult members of society, we know how to acknowledge each other, how to be polite and tactful. All this is taken for granted and makes daily life smooth and predictable. And most of the time we don't think about it unless something goes wrong or we want something more out of others—we want to influence, help, dominate, seduce, teach, learn from, or in some way enter a relationship that is more than mere acknowledgment.

If we want to build a *higher* level of trust because we recognize our dependence on someone or are personally attracted to someone, how do we convey that? How do we show interest? If we want to convey to others that they can trust us, how do we convey that? If we want to be helpful and caring, how do we convey that without unwittingly offending the other by offering something that they don't need or want? If we fall in love, how do we build the relationship? In all of these cases, a key element is to learn to make oneself more vulnerable through Humble Inquiry and personalization. This can be difficult because one risks being snubbed or ignored, which can be humiliating. But it is essential because it shows the other person that you are willing to invest something, to go farther than just a minimum task-oriented relationship. Your self-exposure, your vulnerability is the key ingredient in making the relationship more personal.

## In Summary

Humble Inquiry is necessary if we want to build a relationship beyond rudimentary civility, because we may find ourselves in various kinds of interdependencies in which open, task-relevant information must be conveyed across status boundaries. U.S. culture's emphasis on task performance, interpersonal competitiveness, and telling rather than asking makes it more difficult to be humbly inquiring because that may show weakness and, in fact, makes one vulnerable. But, paradoxically, only by learning to be more humbly inquiring can we build up the mutual trust needed to work together effectively and open up the communication channels. Such opening up can occur around the task itself by becoming more personal. How this process of relationship building works out depends on yet another complexity to be explored in the next chapter—our own intrapsychic dynamics, how open we are willing to be, and how much insight we have into our own cognitive and emotional biases.

---

**QUESTIONS FOR THE READER**

- Think about your work situation. What kind of questions would be considered too personal?

- If you wanted to build more of a trusting relationship with one of your subordinates, how would you go about it? How personal would you be willing to be?

- Think about your occupation. Are you aware of any norms or rules in your occupation about how to relate to people higher or lower in status than you?

- Now take a few minutes just to reflect quietly on what you have learned in general so far.

# 6

## Forces Inside Us as Inhibitors

In order to fully understand the role of Humble Inquiry as a means of building a positive relationship, we have to examine further the complexity of communication. We have to understand how the rules that culture teaches us as to what is and is not appropriate to ask or to tell in a given situation influences our internal communication process. As I have pointed out, being a responsible member of society means the acceptance of the rules of how to deal with each other and how to conduct conversations which show reciprocation, equity, and acceptance of each other's claimed value. When we don't get acknowledgment or feel that we are giving more than we are getting out of conversations or feel talked down to, we become anxious, disrespected, and humiliated. Humble Inquiry should be a reliable way to avoid these negative results in a conversation. So why don't we do it more routinely?

One answer is that sometimes we don't want to build a positive relationship; we want to be one up and win. Sometimes we are tempted to use Humble Inquiry as a ploy to draw the other person out in order to gain advantage, but, as we will see, it is a dangerous ploy because we are likely to be sending mixed signals, and our lack of sincerity may come through. In that instance, we will actually weaken the relationship and create distrust.

A second reason is that there are in all cultures specific rules about what it is *not* OK to ask and/or talk about in any given situation, which requires caution as we try to personalize relationships through Humble Inquiry. Such caution escalates when we are conversing with people from other cultures and if we are trying to decipher what is appropriate openness with respect to authority and trust building. In this chapter I first present an interpersonal model that explores this issue and explains why we send mixed signals, why insincere Humble Inquiry does damage, why interpersonal feedback is so complicated, and how Humble Inquiry can avoid some of these difficulties. Later in the chapter we look at an intrapersonal model that explains why so often even well-intentioned Humble Inquiry goes awry and why it is actually difficult to *access our ignorance*, to ask questions to which we truly don't know the answer.

## The Johari Window: Four Parts of Our Socio-Psychological Self

The Johari window is a useful simplification first invented by Joe Luft and Harry Ingham to explain the complexity of communication.[11] We each enter every situation or budding relationship with a culturally defined *open self*—the topics that we are willing to talk about and know are OK to talk about with strangers—the weather, where you are from, "name, rank, and serial number," and task-related information. We have all learned what is appropriate in a given situation. What we talk about with a sales clerk and what we talk about with a stranger at a party are different but quite circumscribed by the culture. We also develop clear criteria of what is personal and what is not.

As we converse with others, we send a variety of sig-

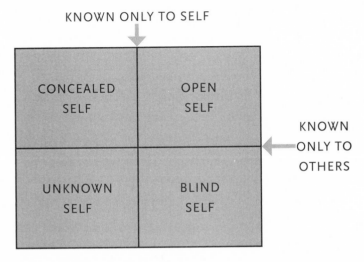

KNOWN ONLY TO SELF

|               | |
| CONCEALED SELF | OPEN SELF |
| UNKNOWN SELF   | BLIND SELF |

KNOWN ONLY TO OTHERS

**The four parts of the self**

nals above and beyond the intentional ones that come from our open self. Our body language, our tone of voice, our timing and cadence of speech, our clothing and accoutrements, our work with our eyes all convey something to the other person, who forms a total impression of us based on all of the data coming from us. Much of this information is passed without our being aware of it, so we must acknowledge that we also have a *blind self,* the signals we are sending without being aware that we are sending them, which nevertheless create the impression that others have of us.

One of the ironies of social life is that such impressions can be the subject of gossip about us by others but may never be revealed to us. We know that we form impressions of others, so must know that they form impressions of us, but, unless we create special circumstances that bend some of the rules of culture, we may go through an entire lifetime without ever finding out what some others really thought of us. This insight introduces us to our *concealed self*—all the things we know about ourselves and others but are not supposed to reveal because it might offend or hurt others or might be too embarrassing to ourselves.

Things we conceal from others are insecurities that we are ashamed to admit, feelings and impulses we consider to be anti-social or inconsistent with our self-image, memories of events where we failed or performed badly against our own standards, and, most important, reactions to other people that we judge would be impolite or hurtful to reveal to their face.

We realize that in a relationship-building process the most difficult issue is how far to go in revealing something that normally we would conceal, knowing at the same time that unless we open up more, we cannot build the relationship. When such opening up is formatted, as in special workshops or meetings designed for the purpose, we label this category of communication *feedback*. The contortions we go through to get feedback mirror the cultural restrictions on not telling others face to face what we really think of them. The reluctance we display when someone asks us for feedback mirrors the degree to which we are afraid to offend or humiliate. We duck the issue by trying to emphasize positive feedback, knowing full well that what we really are dying to hear from others is where they see us as wanting or imperfect, so that we can improve. We see all our own imperfections because our concealed self is filled with self-doubt and self-criticism, and we wonder whether others perceive the same flaws. And, of course, they do, but they would not for the world tell us, in part because that would license us to tell them about their flaws, and we would then both lose our self-esteem.

Asking about and revealing something that is personal

are ways we break out of this cultural straitjacket. We can drop the professional task-oriented self and either ask about or reveal something that clearly has nothing to do with the task situation but that invites acknowledgment and a more personal response. In that sense, Humble Inquiry can begin with something we reveal about ourselves, as a prelude to asking about that area in the other. I can choose to tell something to the other that reveals Here-and-now Humility and thus opens the door to personalizing the conversation. Dr. Brown can tell his team over lunch how much he enjoys fishing in the Scottish Highlands, and Dr. Tanaka can reveal his passion for golf. They can then joke about the tough work schedule and how it prevents them from ever getting any food better than what the hospital cafeteria offers.

If these early revelations and questions are acknowledged and reciprocated, the relationship develops and allows "going deeper." But it has to be a slow and carefully calibrated process. Recall the *New Yorker* cartoon where a blustery boss says to his subordinate, "I want you to tell me exactly what you think of me . . . even if it costs you your job." In other words, a great deal can be exchanged before the relationship gets to the personal feedback stage, and even then it probably works best if it stays on task-related matters. Personal feedback remains dangerous even in an intimate relationship.

In a relationship across hierarchical boundaries it may be necessary for the higher status person to start humble inquiry not with a bunch of personal questions to his team but with a revelation about himself as in the above example with Dr. Brown. Since offending the boss is the bigger risk, it is the boss who may have to define personal boundaries by carefully choosing some things to reveal that then legitimize Humble Inquiry to the rest of the team.

The fourth self—the *unknown self*—refers to those things that neither I nor the people with whom I have relationships know about me. I may have hidden talents that come out in a brand new situation, I may have all kinds of unconscious thoughts and feelings that surface from time to time, and I may have unpredictable responses based on psychological or physical factors that catch me by surprise. I have to be prepared for the occasional unanticipated feeling or behavior that pops out of me.

Now imagine the conversation as a social seesaw with two people getting to know each other, a reciprocal dance of self-exposure through alternately questioning and telling based on curiosity and interest. Gradual self-exposure will occur either through answers to Humble Inquiry or by deliberate revelations. If these early self-revelations are accepted by the other, then gradually more personal thoughts and feelings are put out as a test of whether the other will still react positively to them. In each move, we claim a little more value for ourselves and thereby make ourselves a little more vulnerable. If the other person continues to accept us, we achieve a higher level of trust in each other. What we think of as *intimacy* can then be thought of as revealing more and more of what we ordinarily conceal.

Humble Inquiry functions as an invitation to be more personal and is therefore the key to building a more intimate relationship. Early in a relationship, such invitations can be as basic as the senior surgeon asking the new nurse and technician their names or where they are from, thereby showing interest in them as whole people and not just in their professional roles.

In summary, conversations are inevitably complex because the messages are complex and nuanced even if the sender intends them to be very simple and direct. So even though Humble Inquiry can be defined as an attitude based on your curiosity, asking questions to which you do not know the answers, the implementation is complex because either you are not sure what you should be curious about or your question can be misunderstood. Being curious about and asking about something can easily become too personal and lead the other person to be offended. Therefore, the cultural rules about what is personal and what is intimate have to be understood and followed unless, by mutual agreement, they have somehow been suspended in a "cultural island," a concept that will be explained in the last chapter.

## Psychological Biases in Perception and Judgment—ORJI

What comes out of our mouth and our overall demeanor in the conversation is deeply dependent on what is going on inside our head. We cannot be appropriately humble if we misread or misjudge the situation we are in and what is appropriate in that situation. We must become aware that our minds are capable of producing biases, perceptual distortions, and inappropriate impulses. To be effective in Humble Inquiry, we must make an effort to learn what these biases and distortions are.

To begin this learning, we need a simplifying model of processes that are, in fact, extremely complex because our nervous system simultaneously gathers data, processes data, proactively manages what data to gather, and decides how to react. What we see and hear and how we react to things are partly driven by our needs and expectations. Though these processes occur at the same time, it is useful to distinguish them and treat them as a cycle. That is, we observe (O), we

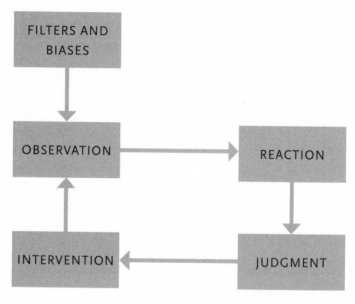

**The ORJI cycle**

react emotionally to what we have observed (R), we analyze, process, and make judgments based on our observations and feelings (J), and we behave overtly in order to make something happen—we intervene (I).[12] Humble Inquiry is one category of such an intervention.

### OBSERVATION (O)

Observation should be the accurate registering through all of our senses of what is actually occurring in the environment and what the demands are of the situation in which we find ourselves. In fact, the nervous system is proactive, programmed through many prior experiences to filter data that come in. We see and hear more or less what we expect or anticipate based on prior experience, or, more importantly, on what we hope to achieve. Our wants and needs distort to an unknown degree what we perceive. We block out a great deal of information that is potentially available if it does not fit our needs, expectations, preconceptions, and prejudgments.

We do not passively register information. We select out from the available data what we are capable of registering and classifying, based on our language and culturally learned concepts as well as what we want and need. To put it more dramatically, we do not think and talk about what we see; we see what we are able to think and talk about.

Psychoanalytic and cognitive theories have shown us how extensive perceptual distortion can be. Perhaps the clearest examples of this are the defense mechanisms *denial* and *projection*. *Denial* is refusing to see certain categories of information as they apply to us, and *projection* is seeing in others what is actually operating in us. It has also been shown that our needs distort our perceptions, such as when our thirst makes us see anything in the desert as an oasis. To deal with reality, to strive for objectivity, to attempt to see how things really are—as artists attempt to do when they want to draw or paint realistically— we must understand and attempt to reduce the initial distortions that our perceptual system is capable of and likely to use.

## REACTION (R)

The ORJI cycle diagram shows emotional reactions occur as a result of what we observe. There is growing evidence that the emotional response may actually occur prior to or simultaneously with the observation. People show fear physically before they perceive the threat. This being the case, the most difficult aspect of learning about our emotional reactions is that we often do not notice them at all. We deny feelings or take them so much for granted that we, in effect, short-circuit them and move straight into judgments and actions. We may be feeling anxious, angry, guilty, embarrassed, joyful, aggressive, or happy, yet we may not realize we are feeling this way until someone asks us how we are feeling or we take the time to reflect on what is going on inside us.

A common example occurs when we are driving and someone unexpectedly cuts in front of us. The momentary sensation of threat is a reaction that makes us observe that the person is cutting us off, which leads first to the instant judgment that (s)he has no right and then to the intervention that we speed up to prevent it or pull up even at the next light to shout at the person who cut us off. The instant judgment prevents us from the safer alternative of slowing down to allow the other car in.

Feelings are very much a part of every moment of living, but we learn early in life that there are many situations where feelings should be controlled, suppressed, overcome, and in various other ways deleted or denied. As we learn sex roles and occupational roles, and as we become socialized into a particular culture, we learn which feelings are acceptable and which ones are not, when it is appropriate to express feelings and when it is not, when feelings are "good" and when they are "bad."

In our task-oriented pragmatic culture we also learn that feelings should not influence judgments, that feelings are a source of distortion, and we are told not to act impulsively on our feelings. But, paradoxically, we often end up acting *most* on our feelings when we are least aware of them, all the while deluding ourselves that we are carefully acting only on judgments. And we are often quite oblivious to the influences that our feelings have on our judgments.

It is not impulsiveness per se that causes difficulty—it is acting on impulses that are not consciously understood and hence not evaluated prior to the action that gets us into trouble. The major issue around feelings, then, is to find ways of getting in touch with them so that we can increase our areas of choice. It is essential for us to be able to know what we are feeling, both to avoid bias in responding and to use those feelings as a diagnostic indicator of what may be happening in the relationship.

Practicing Humble Inquiry before we judge and act becomes an important way of preventing unfortunate consequences. Recall the story of the student who shouted at his daughter for interrupting his studying instead of *asking* her why she had knocked on his study door. An important use of Humble Inquiry in this regard is to inquire of oneself before one acts. Ask yourself, "What am I feeling?" before you go to judgment and action. If the driver had asked that question before speeding up, he or she might have recognized the sense of threat and followed up with, "Why am I so foolish as to risk an accident when I don't even know why this other driver is in such a hurry?"

## JUDGMENT (J)

We are constantly processing data, analyzing information, evaluating, and making judgments. This ability to analyze prior to action is what makes humans capable of planning sophisticated behavior to achieve complex goals and sustain action chains that take us years into the future. The capacity to plan ahead and to organize our actions according to plan is a unique aspect of human intelligence.

Being able to reason logically is, of course, essential. But all of the analyses and judgments we engage in are worth only as much as the data on which they are based. If the data we operate on is misperceived or our feelings distort it, then our analysis and judgments will be flawed. It does little good to go through sophisticated planning and analysis exercises if we do not pay attention to the manner in which the information we use is acquired and what biases may exist in it. Nor does analysis help us if we unconsciously bias our reasoning toward our emotional reactions. It has been shown that even under the best of conditions we are only capable of limited rationality and make systematic cognitive errors, so we should at least try to minimize the distortions in the initial information input.

The most important implication is to recognize from the outset that our capacity to reason is limited and that it is only as good as the data on which it is based. Humble Inquiry is one reliable way of gathering data. For example, when I perceive someone in need of help lying on the sidewalk, before reaching down to help them up I should ask, "Do you need help, how can I help you?" Or, if my boss has told me after the meeting, "That presentation didn't go well," ask, "Can you tell me a little more, what aspect are you referring to?" before you leap into defensive explanations.

### INTERVENTION (I)

Once we have made some kind of judgment, we act. The judgment may be no more than the decision to act on emotional impulse, but that is a judgment nevertheless, and it is dangerous to be unaware of it. In other words, when we act impulsively, when we exhibit what we think of as knee-jerk reactions, it seems as if we are short-circuiting the rational judgment process. In fact, what we are doing is not short-circuiting but giving too much credence to an initial observation and our emotional response to it. Knee-jerk reactions that get us into trouble are interventions that are judgments based on incorrect data, not necessarily bad judgments. If someone is attacking me and I react with instant counterattack, that may be a very valid and appropriate intervention. But if I have misperceived and the person was not attacking me at all, then my counterattack makes me look like the aggressor and may lead to a serious communication breakdown.

The main reason why Humble Inquiry becomes such an important skill is that genuine curiosity and interest minimizes the likelihood of misperception, bad judgment, and hence, inappropriate behavior. In the culture of Tell, the biggest problem is that we don't really know how valid or appropriate what we tell is to the situation. If we want to build a relationship with someone and open up communication channels, we have to avoid operating on incorrect data as much as we can. Checking things out by asking in a humble manner then becomes a core activity in relationship building.

Reflective reconstruction of the ORJI cycle often reveals that one's judgment is logical but is based on "facts" that may not be accurate; hence the outcome may not be logical at all. It follows, therefore, that the most dangerous part of the cycle is the first step, where we take it for granted that what we perceive is valid enough to act on. We make attributions and prejudgments rather than focusing as much as possible on what really happened and what the other person really meant. The time where Humble Inquiry is often most needed is when we observe something that makes us angry or anxious. It is at those times that we need to slow down, to ask others in a humble way in order to check out the facts, and to ask ourselves how valid our reaction is before we make a judgment and leap into action.

## In Summary

When we consider the two communication models together, we can see that even ordinary conversation is a complex dance involving moment-to-moment decisions on what to say, how to say it, and how to respond to what the other says. What we choose to reveal is very much a product of our perception of the situation and our understanding of the cultural rules that apply in that situation. Our initial biases in what we perceive and feel, how we judge situations, and how we react all reflect our culture and our personal history. We are all different because we have different histories both culturally and personally. And, most importantly, our perceptions of our roles, ranks, and statuses within a given situation predispose us to assume that we know what is appropriate. Situations in which participants have different perceptions of their roles, ranks, and statuses are, therefore, the most vulnerable to miscommunication and unwitting offense or embarrassment. It is, in fact, a miracle that we communicate as well as we do.

Common language based on a common culture helps. Insight into the complexities as described in this chapter helps. And a bias toward asking before telling or leaping into action helps. The reason asking is a strength rather than a weakness is that it provides a better chance of figuring out what is actually going on before acting.

If the tasks that society faces are becoming more complex and interdependent, and if the problem solvers working on these tasks are increasingly of different ranks, statuses, and cultures, the ability to ask in a humble way will become ever more important. In the final chapter, I provide some guidelines to become more proficient in this complex task of Humble Inquiry.

## QUESTIONS FOR THE READER

- Think about a recent conversation. Ask yourself whether you were picking up different messages from what the person was saying (open self) and what you were sensing (blind self)?

- Now think about yourself: what signals might you be sending from your blind self?

- Reveal to your spouse, partner, or good friend what you think are signals that you send from your blind self. Ask for comments, elaboration, and clarification so that you can learn more about your own communications.

- Think back over recent events and try to recall an incident when you acted inappropriately. Reconstruct what went wrong—inaccurate observation, inappropriate emotional reaction, bad judgment, or unsuitable action. Ask yourself where in the cycle you could have taken corrective action.

- Now take a few minutes just to reflect quietly on what you have learned in general so far.

# 7

## Developing the Attitude of Humble Inquiry

**The skills of Asking** in general and Humble Inquiry in particular will be needed in three broad domains: 1) in your personal life, to enable you to deal with increasing cultural diversity in all aspects of work and social life; 2) in organizations, to identify needs for collaboration among interdependent work units and to facilitate such collaboration; and 3) in your role as leader or manager, to create the relationships and the climate that will promote the open communication needed for safe and effective task performance.

The attitudes and behaviors required in each of these three areas are to some degree countercultural and will, therefore, require some unlearning and new learning. In particular, some broadening of perception and insight will be needed to help you identify when and where you might do less *telling* and more *asking*. I believe that we will all need to think more broadly and deeply about the role of relationships in the complex and diverse world of the future, which will require much more use of Humble Inquiry in the building of such relationships.

In the recent and very timely book *Dancing at the Edge,* the authors propose that to live in the 21st century will require a new kind of human being, one that is more conscious of self, more social, more culturally wise, and more innovative in taking action.[13] They further propose that all of us already have the capacities for the personal growth that will be needed. I concur with this point of view and believe we are all able to be more humble and more inquiring. So what are we to do?

## The Two Anxieties of Unlearning and New Learning

Learning new things is easy when there is no unlearning involved. But if the new learning, the attitude of Humble Inquiry, has to displace some old habits of Telling, two anxieties come into play that have to be managed. What I call *survival anxiety* is the realization that unless we learn the new behavior, we will be at a disadvantage. Survival anxiety provides the motivation to learn. But as we confront the learning task and develop new attitudes and behavior, we realize it may be difficult, or we may not want to tolerate the period of incompetence while we learn, or our friends may not understand or welcome our new behavior. Anticipating all these potential difficulties is *learning anxiety* and causes resistance to change. As long as learning anxiety remains stronger than survival anxiety, we will resist change and avoid learning.

One might argue then that in order to learn, one must increase survival anxiety, but this only increases our overall tension. To facilitate new learning, we need to *decrease learning anxiety*. We have to feel that the new behavior is worthwhile, that it is possible to learn, that there will be guidance, coaching, and support to get us started, and that there will be opportunities to practice. If what we are learning is somewhat countercultural, we have to provide those supports ourselves. So what might be some ways of supporting ourselves in the process of learning to be more humble and more inquiring?

## SLOW DOWN AND VARY THE PACE

Let's go back to the relay race example: when you start your lap, it is appropriate to run as fast as possible. But when you enter the baton passing area, you have to decelerate, reach out with the baton, wait until it is firmly grasped, and then jog off to rest and prepare for the next race. The person to whom you passed the baton must start accelerating in coordination with your decelerating, stick out his or her hand, wait for the baton to be handed over, grasp it firmly and then run as fast as possible until the next baton passing area. The culture of Do and Tell does not teach us how to change pace, decelerate, take stock of what we are doing, observe ourselves and others, try new behaviors, build new relationships.

In my personal life, especially as I am aging, I find that the biggest mistakes I make and the biggest risks I run all result from mindless hurrying. If I hurry, I do not pay enough attention to what is going on, and that makes mistakes more likely. More importantly, if I hurry, I do not observe new possibilities. Learning Humble Inquiry is not learning how to run faster but how to slow down in order to make sure that I have observed carefully and taken full stock of situational reality. It's making sure that the baton pass is successful. In the rapid pace of work, can we take brief time outs, make time for coffee breaks, or chat at the water cooler or copying machine and engage in a little Humble Inquiry at those moments?

If successful task accomplishment requires building a new relationship with a colleague on whom I will be dependent, how long will that actually take? Personalizing the relationship, doing something informal together such as meeting for lunch or dinner need not be a big time consuming production. If Dr. Brown really wants his surgical team to communicate effectively with him, all he has to do initially is to bring them together in a less formal setting and ask them on a more personal basis to discuss with him how they can best work together. The essential act of Humble Inquiry is in bringing them together and getting interested in them as people before asking them to help create a good climate of communication. It need not take much time, but it takes a different pace. Any leader can do that.

The learning stage where a relationship is being built requires slowing down and building trust, but once the relationship has been built, work actually gets done much faster.

## REFLECT MORE AND ASK *YOURSELF* HUMBLE INQUIRY QUESTIONS

In our task-oriented impatient culture of Do and Tell, the most important thing to learn is how to reflect. We won't know when it is essential to be humble and when it is appropriate to tell unless we get better at assessing the nature of the situation we are in, what the present state of our relationships with others is, and, most important, what is going on in our own head and heart. One way to learn to reflect is to apply Humble Inquiry to ourselves. Before leaping into action, we can ask ourselves: What is going on here? What would be the appropriate thing to do? What am I thinking and feeling and wanting? If the task is to be accomplished effectively and safely, it will be especially important to answer these questions: On whom am I dependent? Who is dependent on me? With whom do I need to build a relationship in order to improve communication?

## BECOME MORE MINDFUL

Reflection implies becoming more *mindful*. The best way to explain Ellen Langer's important concept of *mindfulness* is through recounting my eye-opening experience with her.[14] One summer at Cape Cod my son's little girl Stephanie cut her head on a glass table. There were no doctors immediately available so we had to get in the car and drive for a couple of hours to the nearest hospital. We waited for another hour, got the cut stitched up, drove two hours back to our cottage, and finally got to bed at two a.m. The next morning my wife Mary and I met Ellen at the Provincetown tennis courts and told her about our awful evening. She gave us a long look and asked, "Well, what *else* was happening all this time?" We were blank for the moment but she pursued with, "As I understand it, you were with your granddaughter from eight p.m. to two a.m. *What else* was happening all this time?" And then our fog lifted. In the car and during all of this waiting time Stephanie had been cheerful, chatty, and delightful. We had had six quality hours with her and had let our self-pity about the late hour wipe out savoring this great experience.

What Ellen reminded us of was that we take in a great deal of data, but our tendency to leap to judgment prevents us from reflecting on most of it. So her question, "What else is happening?" should become an important mantra not only for reflecting but also for instant assessment of situations that we are entering. Humble Inquiry presumes accurate assessment of the situation, so asking ourselves what else is happening is essential. Paradoxically this involves learning to be humble with respect to ourselves—to honor our human capacity to take in and deal with complexity, to have a broad range of experiences, and to be agile in responding to those experiences. The tough boss who has always relied on telling, may find, upon reflection, that he or she has the capacity and even the desire to try a different approach, to go to a subordinate and in a kindly way say: "What are you working on? Tell me about it . . ."

## TRY INNOVATING AND ENGAGE THE ARTIST WITHIN YOU

Becoming reflective and broadening our capacity to see and feel more is difficult because culture does script us to such a high degree. To break out of these scripts we need to engage the arts and our own artistic impulses. Artists learn to expand themselves—to see more, to feel more, to do more. In the case of theater and acting, they learn through trying on new roles. In the case of painting, they learn the discipline of seeing accurately what is out there before they try to render it. They learn new theory in working with color and learn new motor skills in wielding a pencil or a brush. The impact of this was brought home to me when I attended a watercolor class for a group of unemployed, previously homeless, and drifting adults. I watched how these twelve people grew in front of my eyes as they were instructed to do simple brushstrokes and witnessed their own ability to put paint on paper and have it look like something.

Doing something artistic expands mind and body. It is not about whether it is any good or not; it is about trying something really new that is ego expanding. I think there is an artist in every one of us, but we don't honor the creative part of ourselves enough. A well-timed Humble Inquiry that launches a conversation that leads to a relationship should be thought of as a thing of beauty. Innovations in how we conduct conversations should be treated as art. In a strategy meeting of 70 health care executives, my colleague, Ilene

Wasserman, was asked to create an event that would get these executives into some kind of relationship with each other in order to implement the new plan. She divided them into random pairs and gave the instructions that when they had sat down together, either one should start by saying, "So . . . what about you . . . ?" Brilliant and artistic.

Nothing is more stultifying than running a meeting by Robert's Rules of Order and to impose the political process of majority rule on small working groups where total commitment is needed. When I opened the meeting of my task force on the capital campaign by asking each member to tell us why he or she belonged to this organization, this turned into a conversation that was beautiful. It amazes me how often a low-key question along the lines of "How do each of you feel about the direction we are going in?" produces far better decisions than motions, seconds, and votes. There is growing recognition that the complex work of today is better likened to improvisation theater and jazz bands than to formal bureaucratic models of organization. There is no substitute for doing something creative even if it is only doodling, keeping a journal, or writing meaningful letters to friends and relatives. Even e-mails can be beautiful, and blogs are clearly drawing on our artistic sense.

Accessing your own aesthetic sense is not difficult. All you have to do is to go to the theater, visit the local museum, and, above all, travel. As the world becomes more culturally diverse, nothing is more important than to experience other cultures and discover how many ways humans have discovered to live. Most of my important lessons about life have come from recognizing how others from a different culture view things. In the world of Google, we don't even have to go physically. It amazes me how much I can travel and experience art even on the Internet.

## REVIEW AND REFLECT ON YOUR OWN BEHAVIOR AFTER AN EVENT

If you learn to slow down, vary your pace, and become more mindful and creative, you will also have time for a particular form of reflection, which is to review and analyze something that you have just done. Effective groups review their decisions to see what can be learned. When the army does maneuvers, it does an after-action review in a deliberate attempt to get feedback from everyone regardless of rank. Hospitals hold special meetings to review cases, especially when things go wrong.

The power of a process review period is that the boss can suspend the cultural rules of deference and ask even the lowest-ranking people in the group to speak frankly about their perceptions of what has gone on. In those reviews, Humble Inquiry is the primary form of question to elicit accurate information from everyone. The review ends with a listing of what everyone learned. As the questions at the end of the chapters suggest, you should keep such a list for yourself based on your own review of your behavior.

## BECOME SENSITIVE TO COORDINATION NEEDS IN YOUR WORK

You may be personally comfortable with your own Humble Inquiry skills, but your organization may be underperforming because various employees or groups do not recognize the degree to which they are, in fact, interdependent. There is growing acknowledgment that organizations perform better when the employees in various departments recognize their degree of interdependence and actively coordinate and collaborate with each other. Jody Gittell noted in her research on this issue that the key to coordination is *shared goals, mutual understanding of each other's work,* and *mutual respect.*[15]

If you were the manager of a work group, you would want to use Humble Inquiry to determine the present state of interdependence and then invent processes in which the necessary relationships could be built to increase the level of collaboration. In high-hazard industries, collaboration, open communication, and mutual help become not only a matter of effective performance but also the key to safety, because the mutual respect should include willingness to communicate openly across the *hierarchical* boundaries.

## AS A LEADER, BUILD RELATIONSHIPS WITH YOUR TEAM MEMBERS

The toughest relearning, or new learning, is for leaders to discover their dependence on their subordinates, to embrace Here-and-now Humility, and to build relationships of high trust and valid communication with their subordinates. This kind of attitude and behavior is the most counter-cultural, yet, I believe, the most important to learn.

The various suggestions made in this chapter so far combine to enable you, as a leader, to tackle this challenge. It goes without saying that you will need the insight to see the need for such relationships in the first place. Slowing down, reflecting, becoming more mindful, accessing the artist within you, and engaging in more process reviews—all will lead to a clearer recognition of what the needs for coordination and collaboration are in your work situation.

## BUILD "CULTURAL ISLANDS"

What remains is to devise some innovative ways to actually get the work team together and, through Humble Inquiry, begin to build the necessary trusting relationships. If the team is culturally homogeneous, it is a matter of getting them together in an informal setting and personalizing the conversation. Making yourself vulnerable will elicit a more personal conversation, and through successive rounds of asking, telling, and acknowledging, trust and openness will build to the point where you can ask the difficult question, "If I am about to make a mistake, will you tell me?" You can then assess whether you have achieved the climate of psychological safety in which all of you will help each other and communicate openly. If it still feels uncomfortable, you can humbly ask, "What do we need to do differently to get to that point of perpetual, mutual help?"

A different kind of innovation will be needed when your team members are culturally heterogeneous, as was Dr. Brown's team in the Chapter 1 example. As the leader, you don't know initially what each team member's own culture prescribes as the rules of deference and demeanor and what the boundaries are, both professional and personal. Cultural stereotypes will not help because you don't know whether or not your team member fits the stereotype.

For this kind of relationship building, you need to create a "cultural island," a situation in which you will attempt to suspend some of the cultural rules pertaining to authority and trust relationships. To do this, you need to bring your team together in an informal environment, away from the work setting, around more personal activities such as a meal or a recreational activity. A stodgy Swiss-German company made the centerpiece of its annual meeting of the top three tiers of executives a competition in a sport that no one was any good at—crossbow shooting or some other arcane local sport. The activity brought everyone down to the same status level, which then made it easier to talk more openly and build cross-hierarchical relationships.

If that feels like too much of an investment, you can bring the group together around a long lunch or dinner and ask members to talk specifically about their own experience in dealing with authority and trust. For example, you might ask them to say what they would have done in their own cultural environments if their superiors made or were about to make a mistake. By listening to actual accounts, the team can begin to calibrate where there is common ground, and you, as leader, can begin to sense what you will have to do to elicit open communication.

A similar question for everyone to answer could be, "In your own cultural environment, how did you know whether or not you could trust each other and the boss?" The goal is to elicit behavioral accounts that enable all of the members of the team to experience and calibrate the degree of diversity of rules that are operating. Until you know the range of diverse rules, you have no basis for exploring where there might be common ground that everyone can commit to.

The important point is not to judge each other but to look for common ground. If team members were to indicate that under no circumstances would they tell the boss when a mistake was about to be made, you would have to consider replacing them. What is important in this activity is to create in a learning mode what might happen in the real situation and to build consensus on what to do when surprises occur. You, as the boss, would have to model a Here-and-now Humble stance to help your team members take a risk and be honest with you as to what they would do and what they would commit to in the real work situation.

## Concluding Comment

All of us find ourselves from time to time in situations that require innovation and some risk taking. Some of us are formal leaders; most of us just have leadership thrust upon us from time to time by the situations we find ourselves in. The ultimate challenge is for you to discover that at those moments you should not succumb to telling, but to take charge with Humble Inquiry.

# Notes

1. Edgar H. Schein, *Process Consultation Revisited* (Englewood Cliffs, NJ: Prentice-Hall, 1999).

2. Edgar H. Schein, *Helping: How to Offer, Give, and Receive Help* (San Francisco: Berrett-Kohler, 2009).

3. For this example the gender of the characters reflects the current situation in medicine and is thus intended to reflect current reality rather than what might be desirable.

4. Edgar H. Schein, *Helping: How to Offer, Give, and Receive Help* (San Francisco: Berrett-Koehler, 2009).

5. Edgar H. Schein, *Organizational Culture and Leadership*, 4th ed. (San Francisco: Jossey-Bass, 2010).

6. Stephen Potter, *Gamesmanship* (New York: Holt, 1951) and *One-Upmanship* (New York: Holt, 1952).

7. A. C. Edmondson, *Teaming: How Organizations Learn, Innovate, and Compete in the Knowledge Economy* (San Francisco: Jossey-Bass, 2012).

8. Ibid.

9. Edmondson, personal communication.

10. Melissa Valentine, *Team Scaffolds: How Minimal In-Group Structures Support Fast-Paced Teaming* (Unpublished doctoral dissertation, 2013).

11. Joe Luft, "The Johari Window," *Human Relations Training News* 5, pp. 6–7.

12. Edgar H. Schein, *Process Consultation Revisited* (Englewood, NJ: Prentice-Hall, 1999).

13. Graham Leicester and Maureen O'Hara, *Dancing at the Edge: Competence, Culture and Organization in the 21st Century* (Axminster, Devon: Triarchy Press, 2012).

14.  Ellen Langer, *The Power of Mindful Learning* (Reading, MA: Addison-Wesley, 1997).

15.  Jody Gittell, *High Performance Healthcare* (New York: McGraw-Hill, 2009).

# Acknowledgments

This book has been in the making for several years. Humble Inquiry as a concept was part of my helping book, but it was Jeevan Sivasubramaniam who saw immediately that this should be a book of its own. I resisted for a while but now thank him heartily for his persistent efforts to get me to do the project. I tried many versions on my colleagues at MIT and my consulting friends and am very grateful to all of them for giving me both encouragement and feedback. Among them, the most helpful were Daniel Asnes, Karen Ayas, Lotte Bailyn, David Coughlan, Tina Doerffer, Jody Gittell, Tom Huber, Mary Jane Kornacki, Bob McKersie, Philip Mix, Joichi Ogawa, Jack Silversin, Emily Sper, John Van Maanen, Ilene Wasserman, and the Berrett-Kohler reviewers who provided detailed comments and suggestions.

Concepts and ideas grow out of experience, so I have to give thanks to the many friends, clients, and strangers who exhibited both the good side of how to humbly inquire and the bad side of telling me things at the wrong times or when I was not ready to hear them. I appreciate and learned from both the good and bad.

I want to thank my kids for their encouragement and support as I continued to work and write even as my circumstances would have permitted me to just take it easy and smell the flowers. Finally, I want to thank my new lady friend

Claude Madden who for the last year has lived with my ups and downs as I was trying to finally shape what Humble Inquiry was to be. She was a consistent source of encouragement and support.

*Palo Alto, CA*
*June 2013*

# Index

acknowledgment, basic,
importance of, 79–80
action-oriented questions, 45
anxiety, survival, 100
artistic abilities, engaging
one's, 104–5
asking, 7–8
skills of, 99–100
telling vs., 3–4
ways relationships are built
by, 8–10
assumptions, tacit, 53–54

basic acknowledgment,
importance of, 79–80
basic humility, 11
basic trust, 79–81
blind self, 85

case examples, of
Humble Inquiry
getting commitments, 29–31
getting help from subordinates, 24–26
giving directions, 31
initiating culture
change, 31–33
missing opportunities, 21–24

power of ignorance, 33–34
providing choices, 35–36
succession plans, 27–29
surgical team, 14–18
causes, questions about, 44–45
concealed self, 85
confrontational inquiry, 46–48
confrontational process
inquiry, 49
conversations
Humble Inquiry and, 41–42
for improving communi-
cation, 9
coordination, becoming sensitive to, 106–7
cultural islands, build-
ing, 107–9
culture
hallmarks of, in United
States, 55–58
as inhibitor of Humble
Inquiry, 53–54
national, 77–79
occupational, 77–79
organizational, 77–79
reasons for focusing on
biases in, 61–63
of Tell, 58–61

deference, 69–71

demeanor, 69–71

denial, 91

diagnostic inquiry, 43–46

diagnostic process inquiry, 49

Digital Equipment
    Corporation, 40

economies, trust and
    social, 79–81

espoused values, 53–55

expressive vs. instrumental
    relationships, 72

feedback, communica-
    tion, 86–87

feelings, questions about, 44

gamesman, 60

gamesmanship, 59–60

Gittell, Jody, 106

Here-and-now humility, 10,
    11–13, 54

    feelings of, 19

Humble Inquiry. *See also*
    inquiry; questioning;
    questions

    case examples of, 21–37

    conversations and, 41–42

    culture as inhibitor of, 53–54

    defined, 2

    differentiating types of ques-
        tions and, 19–20

    as form of inquiry, 40–43

    motivation to explore, 2–3

    questions, asking your-
        self, 102

slowing down and, 101–2

humble process inquiry, 49

humility

    surgical team example of
        kinds of, 14–18

    types of, 5, 10–14

hurrying, Humble Inquiry
    and, 101–2

Ingham, Harry, 84

inquiry. *See also* Humble
    Inquiry; questioning;
    questions

    defined, 18–20

    forms of, 39–49

instrumental vs. expressive
    relationships, 72

intervention, 94–95

Johari window, 84–89

judgment, 93–94

Langer, Ellen, 103

leaders

    building relationships with
        team members and, 107

    challenges of, 63–65

learning, 100–101

learning anxiety, 100–101

lifeman, 60

listening, 7–8, 60–61

Luft, Joe, 84

mindfulness, 103–4

motivations, questions
    about, 44–45

national culture, 77–79

new learning, 100

observation, 90–91
occupational culture, 77–79
Olsen, Ken, 40
one-upmanship, 59–60
open self, 84
optional humility, 11, 54
organizational culture, 77–79
ORJI cycle, 89–90
    observation (O), 90–91
    reaction (R), 91–93
    judgment (J), 93–94
    intervention (I), 94–95

personalization
    defined, 74–75
    as relationship build-
        ing, 75–77
person-oriented relation-
    ships, 72–74
Potter, Stephen, 59–60
processed-oriented
    inquiry, 48–49
projection, 91

questioning, as science and
    art, 18–19
questions. *See also* inquiry
    about feelings and reac-
        tions, 44
    about motivations and
        causes, 44–45
    action-oriented, 45
    asking right, 3–4
    confrontational, 46–48
    differentiating types of, and
        Humble Inquiry, 19–20

Humble Inquiry, asking
        yourself, 102
    reasons for learning to ask
        better, 1–2
    systematic, 45–46

rank, status and, 69–71
reaction, 91–93
reactions, questions about, 44
reflection, on one's
        behavior, 106
relationships
    asking and building, 8–10
    building, between humans, 4
    building, between leaders
        and team members, 107
    instrumental vs.
        expressive, 72
    personalization for build-
        ing, 74–77
    person-oriented, 72–74
    task-oriented, 71–73
    ways asking builds, 8–10
relationships, building, 4–5
relative status, 72
role relations
    personal-oriented, 72–74
    task oriented, 71–74

self
    blind, 84, 86
    concealed, 85, 86
    open, 84, 86
    unknown, 86, 88
social economies, 79–81
status
    rank and, 69–71
    relative, 72

survival anxiety, 100
systematic questions, 45–46

tacit assumptions, 53–54
task-oriented relation-
    ships, 71–74
team members, building
    relationships with, 107
Tell, culture of, 58–61
telling, 7–8

trust, 9
    economies, 79–81

U.S. culture, hallmarks
    of, 55–58

values, espoused, 53–55

Wasserman, Ilene, 105

# About the author— In his own words

This book represents a culmination and distillation of my 50 years of work as a social and organizational psychologist. After undergraduate training at the University of Chicago and Stanford, my Ph.D. training at Harvard's Department of Social Relations in the early 1950s was as an experimental social psychologist. I then spent four years at the Walter Reed Army Institute of Research and began a gradual process of becoming more interested in the sociological details of what went on between people in various kinds of relationships.

My first major research was on the indoctrination of military and civilian prisoners of the Chinese Communists (*Coercive Persuasion*, 1961), which led to an examination of such indoctrination in large corporations when I became a professor at the MIT Sloan School of Management in 1956. It seemed obvious that the important thing to study next was the process of interaction of the individual with the organization, which led to the successful coauthored book on this topic—*Interpersonal Dynamics* (coauthored with Warren Bennis, Fritz Steele, David Berlew, and later John Van Maanen, 3rd ed., 1973) and to an integrated text which helped to define the field (*Organizational Psychology*, 3rd ed., 1980).

The indoctrination and socialization research led inevitably to the discovery through a 15-year panel study that in an open society like the United States, individuals will exercise choices and will be able to shape their careers around strong self images or "career anchors" (*Career Dynamics,* 1978; *Career Anchors,* 4th ed., coauthored with John Van Maanen, 2013).

Working with Group Dynamics workshops in Bethel, Maine, and consulting with Digital Equipment Corporation for many years led to the concept of *process consultation* and the important discovery that the best path to helping people learn is not to tell them anything but to ask the right questions and let them figure it out. I first spelled this out in 1969 as a contribution to consultation methodology (*Process Consultation,* 1969; *Process Consultation Revisited,* 1999) and found that it applies in many interpersonal situations, especially when we try to give or receive help.

All of these processes happen within a culture, so a more detailed study of organizational and occupational cultures led to intensive work on corporate culture—how to think about it, how to change it, and how to relate culture to other aspects of organizational performance. With *Organizational Culture and Leadership* (4th ed., 2010) and *The Corporate Culture Survival Guide* (2nd ed., 2009) I helped to define the field.

The role of leaders as both creators of culture and ultimately victims of culture led to more detailed analyses of interpersonal processes and to two empirical studies of organizational cultures—*Strategic Pragmatism: The Culture of Singapore's Economic Development Board* (1996) and *DEC Is Dead, Long Live DEC: The Lasting Legacy of Digital Equipment Corporation* (2003).

The years of consulting, teaching, and coaching inevitably led to the realization that some processes such as Helping were not well understood and often poorly practiced. The book *Helping: How to Offer, Give, and Receive Help* (2009) was thus an attempt both to analyze and improve that process. It was in that analysis that I realized that Humble Inquiry is not just necessary when we give or receive help but is a more general form of asking that builds relationships. I realized further that building positive relationships is at the core of effective communication and getting work done safely and well. But my work on culture showed me, at the same time, why Humble Inquiry is difficult.

The current book *Humble Inquiry* brings together all of these trends in showing how culture and individual behavior interact, and what it will take in the way of countercultural behavior to deal with the changes that are happening in the world.

# Author Awards

Ed has been recognized for his work with the Lifetime Achievement Award in Workplace Learning and Performance from the American Society of Training Directors (2000), the Everett Cherington Hughes Award for Career Scholarship from the Careers Division of the Academy of Management (2000), the Marion Gislason Award for Leadership in Executive Development from the Boston University School of Management Executive Development Roundtable (2002), the Lifetime Achievement Award as Scholar/Practitioner from the Academy of Management (2009), and the Lifetime Achievement Award from the International Leadership Association (2012).

After 48 years at MIT and after losing his wife in 2008, Ed moved to Palo Alto in 2011, where he is retired but still writing. He has three children and seven grandchildren who live in Seattle, New Jersey, and Menlo Park, California. You can reach him via his e-mail at scheine@comcast.net.

Also by Edgar H. Schein

# Helping
## How to Offer, Give, and Receive Help

Edgar Schein analyzes the social and psychological dynamics common to all types of helping relationships, explains why help is often not helpful, and shows how to ensure that assistance is both welcomed and genuinely useful.

*"Schein provides many anecdotes from his consulting practice, and his short, practical book is rich in insights."*
**—Harvard Business Review**

Paperback, 192 pages, ISBN 978-1-60509-856-2
PDF ebook, ISBN 978-1-57675-872-4

With Peter S. DeLisi, Paul J. Kampas, and Michael M. Sonduck

# DEC Is Dead, Long Live DEC
## The Lasting Legacy of Digital Equipment Corporation

Digital Equipment Corporation was one of the pioneering companies of the computer age, yet it ultimately failed. What happened? In a real-life story that reads like a classical tragedy, Schein—who was a high-level consultant to DEC—and his coauthors show that the very culture responsible for DEC's early rise ultimately led to its downfall.

Paperback, 336 pages, ISBN 978-1-57675-305-7
PDF ebook, ISBN 978-1-60509-408-3

**BK**® Berrett–Koehler Publishers, Inc.
San Francisco, *www.bkconnection.com*          **800.929.2929**

## Berrett–Koehler
## Publishers

**Berrett-Koehler** is an independent publisher dedicated to an ambitious mission: *Creating a World That Works for All*.

We believe that to truly create a better world, action is needed at all levels—individual, organizational, and societal. At the individual level, our publications help people align their lives with their values and with their aspirations for a better world. At the organizational level, our publications promote progressive leadership and management practices, socially responsible approaches to business, and humane and effective organizations. At the societal level, our publications advance social and economic justice, shared prosperity, sustainability, and new solutions to national and global issues.

A major theme of our publications is "Opening Up New Space." Berrett-Koehler titles challenge conventional thinking, introduce new ideas, and foster positive change. Their common quest is changing the underlying beliefs, mindsets, institutions, and structures that keep generating the same cycles of problems, no matter who our leaders are or what improvement programs we adopt.

We strive to practice what we preach—to operate our publishing company in line with the ideas in our books. At the core of our approach is stewardship, which we define as a deep sense of responsibility to administer the company for the benefit of all of our "stakeholder" groups: authors, customers, employees, investors, service providers, and the communities and environment around us.

We are grateful to the thousands of readers, authors, and other friends of the company who consider themselves to be part of the "BK Community." We hope that you, too, will join us in our mission.

### A BK Business Book

This book is part of our BK Business series. BK Business titles pioneer new and progressive leadership and management practices in all types of public, private, and nonprofit organizations. They promote socially responsible approaches to business, innovative organizational change methods, and more humane and effective organizations.

# Berrett–Koehler
# Publishers

A community dedicated to creating
a world that works for all

## Visit Our Website: www.bkconnection.com

Read book excerpts, see author videos and Internet movies, read
our authors' blogs, join discussion groups, download book apps, find
out about the BK Affiliate Network, browse subject-area libraries of
books, get special discounts, and more!

## Subscribe to Our Free E-Newsletter, the *BK Communiqué*

Be the first to hear about new publications, special discount offers,
exclusive articles, news about bestsellers, and more! Get on the list
for our free e-newsletter by going to **www.bkconnection.com**.

## Get Quantity Discounts

Berrett-Koehler books are available at quantity discounts for orders
of ten or more copies. Please call us toll-free at (800) 929-2929 or
email us at bkp.orders@aidcvt.com.

## Join the BK Community

BKcommunity.com is a virtual meeting place where people from
around the world can engage with kindred spirits to create a world
that works for all. BKcommunity.com members may create their own
profiles, blog, start and participate in forums and discussion groups,
post photos and videos, answer surveys, announce and register for
upcoming events, and chat with others online in real time. Please join
the conversation!